CONTENTS

ABOUT THE AUTHOR

Julian Clay

Julian has a BSc (Hons) degree in Psychology and Business. He was a top sales performer in Kodak's Office Imaging division and progressed to become part of its senior management team.

Since then he has worked with a number of different types and sizes of company (including multinationals) to help them achieve continued sales growth. His expertise lies in understanding the core sales challenges companies face and helping to increase sales in different, competitive markets. His roles have included sales process, development, coaching, training and interim sales management.

His interest in the psychology of selling encouraged him to become a software solutions provider. He developed the CRM application Forecastmanager, which is available on the Salesforce App Exchange. It helps users interpret subjective information to deliver more accurate and confident sales forecasts in order to improve sales performance.

He is the author of *Successful Selling Solutions,* as well as the co-author of *The Sales Manager's Desktop Guide, Sales Strategy for Business Growth* and *The Mobile Boardroom* (Thorogood publishers).

Contact information:
jclay@salestosuccess.com • www.salestosuccess.com

Thank you

I'd like to thank my wife, Nadia, for her love and support during the writing and editing of this book which I dedicate to her and my sons, Max and Alex.

I'd like to thank Nick Tong for giving me the benefit of his knowledge of digital marketing and advice throughout the book. He made a valuable contribution in helping to write the following chapters:

- Chapter 2 – Creating a digital marketing strategy

- Chapter 6 – Getting the best out of data analytics

- Chapter 9 – The future of digital marketing

He also contributed to the editing process in all of the chapters.

Nick Tong, CEO of CTO on Demand, is a highly organised, solution-focused technologist. He has a successful track record of creating many innovative and award-winning bespoke digital platforms. With 18 years of technical and marketing experience, Nick has worked with many recognised brands including Vodafone, Channel 4, Publicis and Courvoisier.

I'd also like to thank Martin Clay for his advice on Chapter 1, A brief history of digital marketing.

INTRODUCTION

Digital marketing has changed the way companies engage with potential customers when selling their products and services. It allows brands to be promoted in a way that makes people feel engaged in order to help them with purchasing decisions.

Digital Marketing for Business Growth introduces you to ways to connect with your customers in the modern world. This will help you get the best return on your investment from a marketing perspective to maximise your selling opportunities.

The book starts with how digital marketing has evolved. It looks at the importance of creating brand awareness and what changes have taken place in the marketing landscape. It then moves on to discuss ways in which you can get people interested in buying products and services and how companies need to create a digital marketing strategy. This enables them to achieve best practice principles so that they can deliver their marketing goals.

We look at what changes are taking place in digital marketing that you should be aware of and how it can be driven through multi-channels. The importance of including the right content on your website and in your marketing material is also covered.

The book moves on to talk about the impact of technology and how important it is for digital marketing. We look at changes in expectations and how the customer experience has come to define the strength of a business relationship. Online purchasing is also something that has changed consumer behaviour.

Topics like what makes a good website and how it can support your digital marketing are focused on. Ways that you can make your website more interactive will help companies to improve their own digital presence.

We progress with a discussion about how to get the best out of your marketing data analytics from your interaction with search engines like Google. We look at what third-party tools can be used as part of this as well as data analytics for social media networks. Important areas like Search Engine Optimisation (SEO) and Pay Per Click (PPC) are included together with how to get the best out of social influencer marketing, that is, how to gain influence with your target audience.

There is a chapter on how traditional forms of marketing work and which ones can be used as part of marketing campaigns. This involves how companies can promote their products and services using a combination of traditional and digital marketing in order to deliver an effective strategy.

The book progresses to how smaller and medium-sized companies (SMEs) can compete internationally. It focuses on the digital marketing aspects involved in developing a strategy to build a platform to successfully trade in other countries. This is something which has been made easier with the development of the Web and digital marketing.

It requires a great deal of planning to have an international strategy in place. Part of this is about understanding the process involved and using your Government's export experience to help you. You also need to be flexible in your approach and monitor your progress.

Finally we will look at the future of digital marketing. This includes the power of data and how technology's advances can help to increase its speed and capability. Areas like machine learning, artificial intelligence (AI) and augmented reality (AR) are now being used as part of the digital marketing process. We also cover how mobile video and other future trends are being adopted by marketers to try and entice potential customers to use their products and services.

About the book

Digital Marketing for Business Growth is a practical guide to the different elements which define digital marketing. It is designed to act as a refresher for experienced marketers as well as giving an insight to those who are new to the topic. This could include business owners, directors of SMEs, people in a marketing-related role or anyone who is interested in digital marketing and just wants to find out more.

The book offers help and advice in a number of key areas. It covers many of the components that you need to create a digital marketing strategy and includes illustrations in the form of charts, graphs and tables, many of which you can then use to create your own processes.

Some topics are covered in a primary chapter and then mentioned in other chapters in a subsidiary way. For example, creating a digital marketing strategy is covered as a primary topic on its own; it is also part of the discussion about international trading and social media networks in later chapters. This allows a reader to think about different aspects of a topic and how it links to other areas of digital marketing.

Many of the abbreviations used in the book will be well known to digital marketers but not perhaps to people who are new to the topic. That is why the first time that some marketing terms appear in each chapter, the full name is used followed by the abbreviation in brackets. After this, the abbreviation alone is used for the rest of the chapter. This means that readers won't always need to refer back to the glossary at the front of the book.

Digital Marketing for Business Growth offers value in terms of being able to give readers an overview of how digital marketing can be applied as best practice. This will help marketers focus on the main areas which are likely to produce results. It will also help people who are not in a marketing role have a much better appreciation of how digital marketing can be used effectively.

Many of the topics are supported with research from eminent companies and related websites. This helps to create credible evidence and support a particular point of view. The variety of ideas and solutions will enable readers to think about how many of the challenges related to marketing can be solved. It will also enable those in a marketing role (or combining it with another role) to get the best out of the digital marketing process.

Each chapter topic is followed by key questions. These are designed to help marketers think about the strength of their value proposition. At the end of each chapter there is a checklist which gives readers practical advice in relation to the topics covered.

Note

In the book we refer to three types of buyer:

- Someone who buys for a company in the business-to-business marketplace (B2B)

- Someone who buys goods and services in person from a shop (or store) in the business-to-consumer marketplace (B2C)

- Someone who buys online (B2C)

It is important to distinguish between B2B and B2C and the terminology most used to describe the target audience they relate to. Also, in the B2C market, the terms 'customer' and 'consumer' are often interchangeable, so readers should look at the context in which these terms are used. This will help the book's learning points to be interpreted correctly, depending on what type of buyer and market they relate to.

Glossary of sales terms

Term	Meaning
AdWords	**AdWords** are words which can be used as part of the Google AdWords advertising service. This allows users to only pay for advertisements on Google when someone clicks on to their website.
AI	**Artificial intelligence** is the development of computers and machines that learn to think and act like humans. It covers areas like problem-solving, language, reasoning, visual perception and knowledge.
B2B, B2C	**B2B** and **B2C** represent the difference between who companies sell to, i.e. **B2B** is a **business-to-business** relationship while **B2C** is a **business-to-consumer** one. Marketing methods will differ between the two types.
Blog	A **blog** is normally a brief, information-based online communication either on a social media site or a website. It helps to maintain and promote customer loyalty and is normally done in a conversational style.
Call to action (CTA)	A **call to action (CTA)** is a request from a company via its website or by email to respond to an invitation. This could include signing up to a newsletter, calling the company etc.
Campaign marketing	**Campaign marketing** is when a company plans and delivers a marketing campaign to reinforce their value proposition or to promote a particular product or service.
Content marketing	**Content marketing** is a strategic marketing approach focused on the value of the content you use on your website and in campaigns. It can be used to reinforce or change customer behaviour.

Client	A **client** is someone who is currently buying your services or who has done in the recent past.
Consumer	A **consumer** is a buyer but in a B2C context. The term is often used to describe someone who buys goods and services online.
CRM	**Customer Relationship Management** is a model for how companies can manage their customers/clients. It uses technology to provide a database and communication system involving sales, finance, marketing, technical and customer service support.
CTR	A **Click Through Rate** measures the number of times people view an online advertisement compared to how many times they clicked on it.
Customer	A **customer** is referred to as someone who is currently buying products either in a B2B or B2C context (or who has done in the recent past). For continuity, the term customer will be the most used term throughout the book to describe company buyers (B2B) and people who buy products and services in a B2C market.
e-commerce	**Electronic commerce** (or **e-commerce**) is the transfer of business and commercial transactions over the Internet.
Inbound marketing	**Inbound marketing** is a form of marketing which relies on the quality of information on a website and ease of navigation to it in order to attract potential customers.
Influencer marketing	**Influencer marketing** involves the paid marketing of products and services to a target audience who have an influence over what a customer might buy. This could be due to popularity, reputation or a company's expertise.

Keywords	**Keywords** are words and phrases which are typed into a search engine like Google to try and match those on a company's website. Marketers use them as part of the SEO and PPC process to make it easier for people doing a search to find their products and services.
Operating system	A **mobile operating system** is one which is designed for mobile and tablet devices. Apple uses an iOS system whereas Google uses Android.
PPC	**Pay Per Click** is a form of Internet marketing where advertisers pay a fee every time one of their advertisements is opened (or clicked). It is a way of trying to 'buy' visits to a website rather than via SEO (although you can use both options simultaneously).
SEO	**Search Engine Optimisation** is the structure and promotion of digital marketing in the form of non-payable (organic) search engine results. It is designed to improve a website's rankings and drive 'traffic' to it.
SEM	**Search Engine Marketing** involves a payable promotion on your website to improve your Search Engine Results Pages (SERPs). It can use SEO and PPC to support this.
SME	**Small and medium-sized enterprise** Small – up to 50 employees Medium – between 50 and 250 employees
SMS, MMS	**Short Message Service** and **Multimedia Messaging Service** are both types of text messaging. The difference is that while an SMS is text only, an MMS allows users to send pictures, photos, video and audio files.

Social media	**Social media** is the group of online communication platforms used to create a 'community' of business and social interaction, for example Facebook, LinkedIn and Twitter. Although they differ in content, collectively they focus on areas like social networking, blogging and forums.
Spam	**Spam** is the term used for unsolicited messages, which are often sent randomly over the Internet to large numbers of users. It is also referred to as junk mail.
The Web	The **World Wide Web** is a collection of servers that support specially formatted documents in a mark-up language called HTML (HyperText Markup Language). It supports links to other documents, – as well as graphics, audio and video files – and allows you to go from one document to another. The Internet is a massive networking infrastructure connecting millions of computers together globally through a variety of languages known as protocols.
USPs	**Unique Selling Points** are factors which add value and differentiate you from a competitor.
Website traffic	**Website traffic** refers to web users who visit a website.
White paper	A **white paper** is an indepth document which helps a reader to understand the issues about a particular subject.

ONE
A BRIEF HISTORY OF DIGITAL MARKETING

CHAPTER TOPICS

- What is digital marketing?
- Changes in the landscape
- Brand awareness

Introduction

Digital marketing has changed the way in which companies market their brands. Every day, companies and individuals are presented with all types of promotions, for example advertising on social media networks and online advertising through to mobile and business applications. This chapter defines the components that make up digital marketing and examines the ways in which marketing has changed over the past few years with the development of technology.

It looks at the brief history of how the (World Wide) Web enabled companies to think digitally. Marketers had a new way to target companies (in a B2B market) and potential customers (in a B2C market) to promote their products and services compared to traditional marketing.

The chapter will cover how digital marketing has changed the way marketers and customers operate. This has distinct advantages to both parties in the way that products and services are bought and sold. Finally it looks at the importance of brand awareness and how you can develop this into customer loyalty. This involves articulating value as well as trying to get potential customers to make a connection with your brand.

What is digital marketing?

Digital marketing is a way of promoting a company's products and services through different channels. The goal is to build interest from a target audience by sharing information designed to attract and engage with them. This is designed to encourage them to purchase something and be an advocate of that brand. There are various means by which digital marketing communicates with its potential target audience including:

- Search Engine Optimisation (SEO)

- Pay Per Click (PPC)

- Search Engine Marketing (SEM)

- Content marketing

- Influencer marketing

- E-commerce

- Social media (Facebook, LinkedIn, Twitter)

- Campaign marketing

- Direct email marketing

Note: The glossary at the front of this book defines many of the above terms.

The different elements which make up digital marketing can be illustrated in the following way:

ELEMENTS OF DIGITAL MARKETING

Although digital marketing has been around since the 1980s, it hasn't always been clearly defined. It focuses on the Web as its core channel of communication and, for many, a company's website is the starting point for digital marketing awareness. Data collection is a key part of the process in order to find out which target companies and people might be interested as potential buyers in the future.

It is worth noting, that in 2016 approximately 3.5 billion people used the Internet. Also over 50 per cent of the world's population who use a mobile phone, access the Internet from it (statista.com). With this in mind, it is not surprising that the rise in digital marketing has taken place. The Web has become a master communication tool used to both send and receive information globally.

Digital marketing uses this power to enhance campaigns which can be viewed in real time. Response rates and the number of purchases made can be viewed as part of any campaign analysis. For this reason, many companies create digital marketing strategies to build potential new business relationships with companies and individuals that previously could not have been targeted in this way.

Technology has allowed buyer and seller to meet each other through a 'virtual' marketplace. It enables companies to create more advanced databases so that communication with a target audience becomes easier to manage.

Where did it come from?

The possibility of digital marketing came with the introduction of the IBM personal computer in the 1980s along with the ability for PCs to store more information. This enabled better storage of relevant information about particular companies and people who were targets for products and services.

'The Web' was invented by Tim Berners-Lee and Robert Cailliau in 1990. They wrote a joint proposal in which the term 'World Wide Web' was used for the first time. By 1991, Tim Berners-Lee had written the first web browser. This revolutionised communication by allowing text documents to be annotated with Hypertext Mark-up Language (HTML) and web pages that could use images and video. Customer Relationship Management (CRM) software was another emerging platform which enabled companies to improve their marketing strategies.

Digital marketing began in its current format with the introduction of the Internet and Web 1.0 platforms. Although this wasn't a particularly interactive platform, it did allow users to get much information from the Web. Another element to its growth was the search engine. For example, by 1995 Internet Explorer was introduced by Microsoft and Google started its own search engine in 1998 and its browser, Chrome, in 2008.

This was soon followed by a rise in social media sites which allowed companies to communicate directly with potential new customers. Once this was possible, the next step was to develop a web marketing strategy to 'tap in' to these new digital platforms.

Google started to improve its search engine and look at ways in which Search Engine Optimisation (SEO) could be utilised to improve a company's ranking on its site. This could be done with Google AdWords (a service to enable companies to display advertisements on Google) and by using algorithms to help prioritise search results. This is covered in *Chapter 6, Getting the best out of data analytics*.

Other elements which helped the digital marketing process evolve included the use of 'cookies'. These allow companies to collect user data and are popular with suppliers like Amazon who can offer consumers products based on previous searches that they have made.

When the Web 2.0 came out it in 1999 it had the advantage of being interactive, with different platforms and networks which allowed users to interact with each other. Social media sites like LinkedIn (which started in 2002) and Facebook (which started in 2004) enabled conversations to take place and groups to be formed. By 2005 YouTube had been introduced and allowed users to watch or post videos on its website (it was bought by Google in 2006).

In 2007 Apple introduced the iPhone which transformed the mobile phone market. It used a mobile web browser along with a touch screen and the ability to download 'applications' or apps (software programs associated with mobile phone and tablet use).

The way digital marketing grew was helped by the ability for Internet users to browse online. This enabled them to make more informed choices and better purchasing decisions by doing research on products and services. By the mid 2000s, this had caused the relationship between many buyers and sellers to change. Buyers in both the B2B and B2C markets had more knowledge about potential purchases, which caused many companies to rethink the way they sold their products and services. Mobile phones accelerated this process as the Internet could be accessed remotely.

Areas like marketing automation enabled companies to launch multi-channel campaigns as well as segment their audience. This meant that they could target specific groups or individuals in a digital format. Customer expectation has risen because of this new-found knowledge. Choice became something which challenged both companies and their potential customers as there was now a common platform for both to be part of. By 2013, advertising on the Web had outgrown investment in newspaper advertising. At this point, only television revenue exceeded Internet advertising spend.

Social media networks like Facebook, LinkedIn and Twitter began to see an increase in advertising revenue from companies investing in digital marketing. By 2014, over one third of this came from B2B vendor Internet sales and this figure is expected to increase.

With digital marketing, campaigns are easier to measure and can reach a larger audience. It can also use a more tailored approach via the Web which enables it to be more interactive than traditional forms of advertising. It also offers a 'two-way' form of communication with potential customers via social media, a website, email etc. as well as being able to get feedback more easily. This has helped companies to put measurement processes in place in order to attract more customers and build brand awareness.

Changes in the landscape

One of the main differences now is that companies have a much wider choice as to how to market their products and services. Communication is another key factor in accelerating change towards digital marketing. Companies can now use a variety of different ways to target potential customers digitally, which were not possible before the introduction of the Web. Also, the speed at which digital technology has advanced has been significant.

If you look at the news, people now have instant access to a website for up-to-date items. Social media sites like Facebook and Twitter offer instant communication and the sharing of images, all of which can be viewed on a tablet or mobile phone. This has forced many companies to rethink how they market themselves in order to get the best out of any future customer relationship.

The progress of digital marketing

The progress of digital marketing has taken place partly because of technology and also due to demand from customers. Some of the benefits of this include marketers being able to measure the outcomes of marketing campaigns better. For example:

- Better quality data

- The ability to analyse information in relation to customer purchases and in real time

- The introduction of campaign management systems (which can help to automate marketing campaigns and measure outcomes)

All of this helps to improve the way potential customers are targeted. Digital marketing can help to enhance the type of business relationship because it has the potential to reach a wider audience than before. This helps the actual engagement in a more meaningful way as campaigns can be tailored to that company or individual.

'Real-time marketing' gives companies the chance to review outcomes almost immediately. It allows them to change something if it isn't working and react quickly to potential feedback (directly or on social media).

Finally, digital marketing is more cost-effective than traditional forms. The costs of producing brochures or paying for television and radio advertising can be expensive. Also, it can be harder to measure the success of radio advertising compared to forms of digital marketing. That is why the latter has the power to transform a company's quality of communication and get a better return on its investment (ROI).

KEY QUESTIONS

- What areas of digital marketing do you need to primarily focus on?

- What are the key components of your own digital marketing process?

- What order of priority do they have?

Brand awareness

If you are looking to increase the amount of digital marketing you do, brand awareness will be a key area for you to consider. This can be described as how strong a brand is to your target audience and is often the first and most important goal in gaining future customer loyalty. It identifies how well someone can remember a brand and what image or experience this has.

Brand awareness involves trying to get potential customers (whether in the B2B or B2C markets) to be aware of and evaluate products and services. It also tries to identify what makes someone buy something and how to get loyalty and regularity of purchases from them. This does depend on a company's (B2B) or individual's (B2C) buying cycle. Once people like a product and remember a particular brand, then the loyalty they show towards it becomes easier to obtain.

Companies are constantly looking for ways to maintain an edge over their competitors. By having a brand which meets a customer's needs and identifies with them in a special way, you increase your chances of retaining them. This can involve a number of factors including:

- Meeting (and exceeding) the customer's needs

- Price

- Value

- History

- Experience

- Reputation

Brand awareness is important because it helps to influence a buyer's choice. If someone has an awareness of a product or service, it makes it easier for that person to identify with the brand. It can also build trust with a company as its values are linked. It makes it more likely that someone will remember a company's products and services in relation to potential future purchases. Brand awareness makes it easier for companies to differentiate themselves and to link their product features to the value they offer. There are two types of brand awareness:

1. *Aided awareness* (recognition) – when talking about a product category, people recognise a brand from a list

2. *Top of mind awareness* (TOMA)* – when a product category is mentioned, someone thinks first of a particular brand (recall).

BRAND AWARENESS AND RECOGNITION

Companies look for potential new customers to progress from brand awareness and brand recognition through to TOMA. Once a brand is trusted and considered of high value, TOMA is more likely to be achieved. Ideal TOMA is when buyers look for a particular brand name they identify with as a way of pre-determining purchasing criteria.

Whether recognition or recall play a stronger role in purchasing decisions can depend on whether you sell a product or a service.

For example, if a product is physically seen then brand awareness will probably play a stronger role in the customer choice. If you sell a service, then brand recall is probably more significant.

There are a number of reasons which affect someone's particular attachment to a brand including:

- A change in taste

- Changes in fashion

- Changing needs

- A change in perception (sometimes caused by another brand becoming more popular).

While some brands have a common need over time, others can be overtaken by more modern technology or changes in taste. Brand awareness and loyalty are key drivers for decision-making about marketing spend and this is important because it will affect a company's potential sales.

Other factors which have affected brand awareness since digital technology was introduced include the globalisation of products and their higher level of homogenisation. This was predicted by T Levitt in The Globalization of Markets (*Harvard Business Review*, 1983). He pointed out the benefits not only of globalisation but also of standardising products and the way they were promoted. He also believed that, by looking for common needs and common values, companies would find it easier to sell profitable products which would enhance their corporate sales performance.

With the growth of technology, digital marketing needed to rise to new challenges. Levitt argued that the combination of technology and globalisation would shape buyer behaviour and preference. This would also impact on the 'economic realities' that companies would face. He predicted that there would be a convergence of products to a point where differentiation became more difficult. This has already

6/2423585

happened and you only need to look at the Apple iPhone, which was quickly copied by other mobile phone manufacturers, as an illustration of this.

This particular point raises the importance of trying to be first in a particular market if you can to build a unique and very attractive brand. However, if you can't articulate areas of high value you may have to lower the price! This is why differentiation becomes more challenging if there is little or no perceived value.

How can you build brand awareness?

In order to build a brand there are a number of areas you can examine, including:

1. A brand which is easy to identify with
Think about the visual element of this along with the 'story' behind the brand and its value to a potential customer.

2. Developing and updating your website
To many companies, a website is their 'shop window'. With this in mind ensure that yours is up to date, relevant and articulates the value of your products and services rather than only the features you offer.

3. Personalisation
By personalising your website you make it easier for people to identify with your brand and to buy from you. It helps to put the customer at the centre of the marketing focus rather than the product offering alone. The two are linked, but it is the customer who is the prime target to please in order for the product and value to be understood.

4. Referrals

One of the best ways to gain more customers and reinforce brand awareness is through referrals or personal recommendations. This can be helped by having innovative products and by great customer service (and account management if you are selling B2B). From a supplier's point of view, there is nothing better than someone you know telling you how good a particular product or service is. It's an endorsement which is easy to relate to and can make purchasing decisions easier.

It can influence a potential new buyer because someone they know has taken the risk to buy. This, to some extent, lessens any fears they might have about the product not working or not being of the quality or value they expected.

5. Social media

Social media can help you to build your brand by promoting the following areas:

- To help communicate trends to potential buyers

- To measure statistics to inform

- To encourage interaction and involvement with your products and services

- As a way of advertising the brand

- To communicate knowledge and up-to-date relevant information

- To promote a unique brand identity which articulates Unique Selling Points (USPs)

Social media can also help to develop a potential buyer's thinking from 'interest to commitment', from 'sceptic to believer' and from liking to 'defending your brand'. This is a powerful way of helping to create and maintain brand awareness. Customer loyalty is covered in more detail in *Chapter 3, Changes that impact on the customer experience.*

6. Direct forms of marketing

Communicating your brand directly through digital and traditional methods to potential customers is another positive way of developing the early stages of brand awareness.

Making a connection

When you are looking at ways to create brand awareness, you need to take into account factors like price and the features of a product because the brand needs to be trusted and well liked. You should also look at five key drivers:

1. Awareness

2. Differentiation

3. Value

4. Accessibility (to your products and services)

5. An emotional connection

This can be illustrated in the following way:

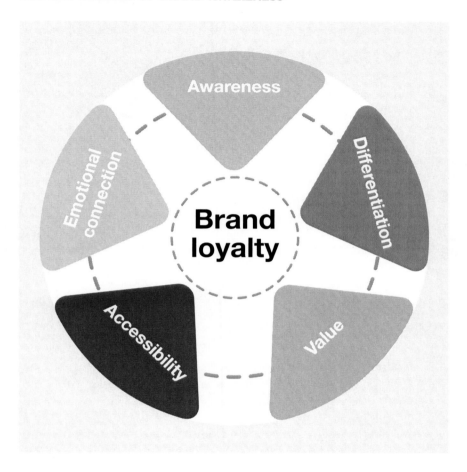

An emotional connection with a brand is perhaps the most important element as it fulfils a customer's needs beyond a level where loyalty is always logical. It is often not transient because a genuine attachment to the product or service takes place.

Chapter summary

Digital marketing has dramatically changed the way in which marketers communicate with their target audience. Companies are better able to reach potential customers through a number of different platforms and channels. This creates greater opportunities to increase awareness, bringing buyer and seller closer and on a mutually beneficial path. It has also led to a much greater amount of customer choice.

Digital marketing has changed how companies plan and execute their marketing campaigns. It has enabled smaller companies to compete in a way which wasn't possible before. This has involved using marketing to build a brand which incorporates social media and digital platforms. It helps to promote value in order to try and make potential customers remember a brand and want to use it. This gives companies a better chance to achieve growth and increase selling opportunities.

Checklist

✓ Look at how different types of digital marketing can help you

✓ Identify the components you need to successfully build your brand

✓ Think about what you need to do to keep your customers loyal

✓ Keep up to date with the changes taking place in your market (blogs, newsletters)

TWO
CREATING A DIGITAL MARKETING STRATEGY

Introduction

A digital marketing strategy is something that can help a company execute its marketing objectives. This chapter looks at the elements needed to define these and turn them into a plan. It includes the type of market you are targeting and areas that can be measured.

Best practice principles need to be agreed and set in a realistic way so that they can be related to the company's overall business objectives. For example, setting up a process to monitor your digital marketing efforts internally and having a marketing team working together towards common goals.

The last section looks at how you can focus on different multi-channels in order to attract new customers and retain them. It involves content you need on your website and material you can produce to attract people to your products and services. You should be mindful of how to attract interest using social media as well as the locality and mobility of your target audience. This will help you to produce an integrated strategy which will make it easier to combine the many facets of digital marketing in a well-structured way.

Marketing goals

Creating a vision for your digital marketing starts with creating goals in which you define the necessary actions a marketing team can develop. In order to attract the right target audience, think about the ways you can prepare, for example:

Target markets

The way you address your potential customers through digital marketing campaigns is important. Get to know the type of market you're targeting so that you:

- Respect the local culture

- Use the right language with your communication

- Find out who the key players are (in B2B target accounts)

- Look at current trends (Twitter is a good resource for this)

- Know what is popular on local radio and television

- Understand what type of mobile devices people use*

---

*smartinsights.com can provide valuable information about mobile marketing statistics

Do a SWOT analysis which measures your **S**trengths, **W**eaknesses, **O**pportunities for future business and potential **T**hreats. You can incorporate this into a PEST analysis in the same way which measures any **P**olitical, **E**conomic, **S**ocial and **T**echnical factors which can affect both you and your competitors.

Technology

Knowing what technology platforms you can take advantage of is an important area to focus on. For example, launching a mobile app in an area with low smartphone adoption is likely to have a relatively low level of success, whereas promoting video content where Internet access is high is more likely to yield good results.

Get organised

Getting well organised should include creating an activity calendar, with key dates and relevant events. Where possible, integrate your own campaign activity into these dates to keep your target audience interested and engaged. This will also help keep your brand relevant.

Objective Key Results

Whatever your objectives are, they should start with interpreting goals the company has at a strategic level. These can then be adapted to include digital marketing. Goals need to be linked to definable actions which can then be communicated to the relevant members of the marketing team. This can be done by creating Objective Key Results or OKRs (which were developed by Intel). They will help to establish and communicate company, team and individual goals and to define measurable results.

Google is a good example of a company that successfully used OKRs early in its trading history as building blocks to drive the company's objectives forward. You should establish what type of return, either in numbers, percentage or value you expect in each particular marketing area. This can be illustrated in the following way with a

B2B example which includes a number of related sales and marketing goals.

BUSINESS-TO-BUSINESS MARKETING GOALS

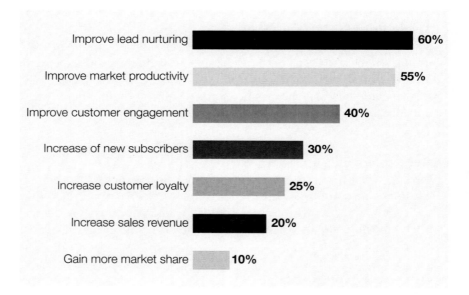

You can then compare the increase you are striving for in each area with real outcomes. Think about the goals from your perspective but, most importantly, from the perspective of your organisation or the people/companies you are targeting. It will enable you to better understand the stages that buyers go through during this process.

Here are examples of a marketing buyer cycle, i.e. the stages that a marketer and a potential buyer might go through.

Marketer	**Buyer**
1. Plan	1. Awareness/discovery
2. Attract	2. Interest
3. Nurture	3. Consideration
4. Convert	4. Commit – Purchase
5. Engage	5. Post-purchase
6. Account manage/retain loyalty	6. Retention (re-purchase)
This is an example of a marketing cycle.	This is an example of a purchasing cycle.

By taking the time to think about things from a buyer's perspective and the process they go through, you will be in a better position to align your goals.

Budget

Part of any investment in digital marketing needs to take into account the budget that is available and how this is going to be spent. Costs can become hard to manage if you don't plan what you are going to invest in and think about how a return is going to be achieved. Be flexible in your approach to this.

Think about what your priorities are and take into account other related expenses that you need to factor in. Look at past digital marketing campaigns and compare the return on investment (ROI). Categorise the different components so that you can see what went well and what didn't go so well. Having a review of this will help you prepare better for the future so that you capitalise on your strengths and learn from any mistakes you made.

Be assertive in admitting if something hasn't worked and encourage others to do the same. It is better to adapt a campaign rather than doing the same things but not getting the results you planned for.

Spending money is always a risk which needs underpinning with good preparation. So, in order to get this right, focus on the quality of what you do and think about the return you are looking for. This will help you avoid the pitfall of trying to save money in areas which prove to be ineffective. This isn't always easy to know in advance but, with good planning, you can maximise the investment of any campaign spend.

KEY QUESTIONS

- What are your marketing goals?

- How well do you implement and track them?

- What OKRs have you set up?

Setting up best practice principles

Creating clearly defined marketing goals is something that some small and medium-sized enterprises (SMEs) might think is best left to multinational companies. But every campaign requires communication with different people in different departments, e.g. sales (converting marketing opportunities) and finance (budget) as well as within a marketing team.

Creating a digital marketing strategy can be seen as a series of stages. It starts by listing these in order to make it a quantifiable proposition. This can be illustrated in the following way:

STAGES OF DEVELOPING A SALES STRATEGY

Digital process	Initial phase	Partially managed goals	Defined strategy	Objective measurement
1 **Strategy**	Plans only	Some managed goals	Defined digital marketing strategy	Strategy fully functional
2 **Performance indicators**	No OKRs	Understanding of types of OKR	OKR measurement now exists	Integrated OKRs
3 **Internal communication**	Limited	Exists but largely un co-ordinated	Defined and part of companypolicy	Aligned to company's business plan
4 **Marketing resources**	Not defined	Aware of and partly working	Defined and working	Balance assessed and optimised
5 **Data**	Limited database	Data capture but not fully co-ordinated	Integrated database with internal systems	Data working, integrated and updated
6 **Customer interaction**	No integrated website	Limited desktop or mobile support	Defined integration of digital platforms	Integrated web, mobile, email and social media

By doing this you will be in a better position to affect the outcomes that determine your success. There are several factors which help with this, including:

- The company's infrastructure and ability to deliver the goals

- The content and way you communicate it

- The team who delivers it

- What metrics you decide to use as part of a measurement process

Look at the elements which define the strategy

It can be tempting to engage with different areas of digital media and social media networks without thinking through the end result. Managing campaigns and segments on a number of platforms or channels can compromise your message consistency. This means it is worth researching how to get the best out of each one you plan to target to support this.

Mistakes can happen if you don't engage in the right areas and in the right way. Some actions you can take to hone your own digital marketing effectively include:

- Interactive web design and content including making it 'mobile friendly'

- A high focus on the content of your website and campaigns (content marketing)

- The use of video

- Think about how to use new features and updates in social media (i.e. Twitter search engine)

- Making a potential customer's online experience more interactive

Keeping up with trends in digital technology will help to ensure that these types of areas can be used to their best effect. Also, being part of a marketing-driven company which can work together to convert the business and sales goals will increase your chances of success.

Think about what best practice looks like and adhere to it. Don't ignore or delay using digital marketing techniques in order to get the most out of your marketing generally, for example:

- Engage in aspects of mobile marketing

- Use good quality graphics on your website and in your marketing campaigns

- Don't use too many keywords as part of a Google AdWords campaign in your content marketing

- Drive your target audience to good examples of landing pages

- Don't over-focus on getting potential customers registered

- Invest in social media videos

- Do A/B testing on new features on your website comparing two versions of a web page*

---

*A/B testing or split testing is comparing two versions of a web page to see which one performs the best.

Not adapting as trends change is another important factor that can affect the quality and success of a campaign. If you keep up your efforts in these areas and ensure that you don't become distracted or too busy, you will be more in control of your own destiny. Be aware of what needs to change and involve those who can make it happen. By doing so, you are more likely to focus on what is important rather than what can become urgent. This can happen if you've reacted too late or failed to react at all to something which needed attention.

Getting departments to work towards one goal

Getting people and departments to work together to share and implement common marketing goals can be a challenge. In order to ensure a marketing team (or agency if you outsource this) understands the goals being aimed for, they need to be agreed and communicated. Understand what your target audience really wants and how to communicate brand value. The types of questions you should be asking include:

- Is your messaging clear?

- Have you asked the right questions?

- Are you working towards realistic time frames with your marketing communication?

- Why should someone relate to your marketing message?

- Are the relevant people internally involved?

The challenges and the risks involved in a campaign need to be assessed. They need defining in advance so that they can be managed. It is also important to have the right resources in place as well as providing any relevant training.

Performance incentives

Another area that you should concentrate on as part of your strategy is the value of starting a performance incentive programme. These can be used on any 'ambassador programme', which is where you pay someone to become a spokesperson for your brand who is not an employee. He/she will be an advocate and represent your company because they believe in it and use your products or services.

You need to find out who the biggest influencers are in your market and try and turn them into advocates for your brand. This involves social reach, i.e. how large an influence a brand ambassador has in relation to driving your marketing message. In order to get a good return for this type of engagement, it is often best to pay people less, but give them a bigger bonus based on performance. You can measure this in several ways including:

- Brand reach (how many people you target)

- Open impressions (how many people have seen it)

- Engagement (how many people like it)

- Inbound traffic

- Number of sales

This can drive more engagements with people who are incentivised to broadcast your message. This in turn will help turn your customers into advocates and then potential 'revenue generators'. You might also want to consider a loyalty programme for example, in a B2C market requesting a review rating of a purchase on a sales channel such as Amazon, if you use this method to sell your products.

It is a good way of promoting new products and services to a defined audience who are mostly loyal to your brand. You could give some free products or run a promotion to thank customers. This can help to promote loyalty, give you feedback and improve customer retention.

Multi-channel marketing

Multi-channel marketing looks to create a unified digital experience to communicate your products and services. This will help to mould all your elements of marketing to an online presence. Different channels include:

- Inbound and content marketing (covered in the next sections)

- Your website

- Social media

- Search Engine Optimisation (SEO)*

- Pay Per Click (PPC)*

- Public relations (PR)

- Email

- Video

---

*SEO and PPC are covered in more detail in Chapter 6, Getting the best out of data analytics.

They should all convey the same message so as to be consistent with your brand(s). In order to break this down, let us look at some of these channels in more detail.

Inbound marketing

Inbound marketing is the actual process of promoting a company through:

- Blogs

- Video/podcasts

- E-books

- Articles/newsletters

- White papers

- SEO

- Products

- Social media marketing

Much of this is likely to be generated from your website and serves to attract customers through the different stages of the purchasing cycle. It is designed to attract people who want to buy your type of products and services through a 'call to action' (CTA) for example:

- Sign up to a newsletter

- Buy something from an e-commerce site

- 'Like' something on a Facebook page

- 'Follow' you on a social network platform, e.g. Twitter, LinkedIn

Always be sure to think about what attracts people to your particular channels, what social networks are performing well and what onsite channels are driving better conversion rates.

Content marketing

Content marketing is the actual content used to deliver inbound marketing. The aim of it is to attract and retain a clearly defined audience and, ultimately, to drive customer action leading to future purchases.

In the first few years of digital marketing, the level of sophistication which companies used wasn't as high as it is now. Many would put too much information on their website rather than look to separate the points of value and CTAs. With content marketing you can engage with people on a number of platforms, driving them to find the right acquisition channel. You should monitor the quality of the content you send out and list your goals in relation to this. These can include:

- Brand awareness

- Upsell (to upgrade or add)

- Cross sell (to a different product)

- Customer retention/loyalty

These areas are integral to a digital marketing strategy. Rather than focusing on your products and services alone, look at ways to engage in a conversation about them. This will help promote a more objective discussion, with different opinions on social media, which can help you to gain genuine interest.

All of this will encourage users to come back to your website to gain valuable information. It will also help your company to be seen as helpful and an authoritative source of information. What a website should offer and how to get the best out of it are covered in *Chapter 4, Getting your website to add value.*

The aim of content marketing is to help you communicate with your target audience by producing information which is interesting and of high quality. It has enabled companies to be more target-driven. Good communication with potential customers is a powerful way of understanding their needs in both the B2B and B2C markets.

Effective content on your website and in your marketing campaigns is a good way of getting your message across as well as generating new leads. It helps to gain higher visibility for your website and your company. If you get it right it should provide real value for money, improve your brand reputation and help you to form closer ties with your customers.

Social-local-mobile (SoLoMo)

Social-local-mobile is the integration of social media, local search and mobile technology in relation to search engine results. It is an extension of a hyper-search (a local business search) and can help to produce a set of social media marketing tools.

SoLoMo relates well to companies being able to target people they are looking to engage with (and who use their mobile phones) on social media networks. Advertisements placed by a supplier, on Google for example, can have been bid for, which will place that company higher on a search results page. The data collected from any 'hit' can be used to pinpoint the type of activity that someone is looking for. This is particularly useful for a mobile phone user, if that person has given the search engine provider permission to use their location.

Consider, for example, a group restaurant owner who pays for PPC in Google and targets people within a close proximity to the restaurant with a key word search. The restaurant will acquire the advertising space which should drive more relevant potential customers to them. The local nature of this will improve the chances of these people knowing the area, location and possibly even the restaurant.

If this is followed up by an actual visit and a positive experience from someone, the restaurant can acquire not only a new customer but a potential brand advocate. This shows the strong link between targeted digital marketing, attracting new customers and customer retention.

Local search

Another way to appear nearer the top of a search engine, particularly if you are not ranking well, is to use 'local search'. This is more relevant if you are looking to attract business on a local or regional level rather than a national or international level. For example, the goal might be to be listed in the top three companies of a Google local search, a '3-Pack'.

This type of search offers clear citations, the name, address and telephone number of the company. With this in mind, you should always include these elements when you have your company's contact details on a third-party website page. They should also be kept in the same format as this will allow search engines to more easily identify your company as one within a particular location. Whenever a citation is obtained, it is a good idea to keep this logged. Then, if you move your company location, you know which directories have been used so that you can update this information.

A local search makes it easier for potential customers to find you and for them to use your website and contact details to get in touch. You may then be only one step away from obtaining a potential new customer!

Integrating your digital marketing

As part of multi-channel marketing, bring all of the main components of digital marketing listed here together so that they are integrated. This can involve key elements like:

- *Managing* your presence in the market place

- *Targeting* of potential customers

- *Measurement* of your goals and performance

- *Content* (and inbound) marketing

- *Engagement* with potential customers

- *SoLoMo* with different mediums and channels

This can be illustrated in the following way:

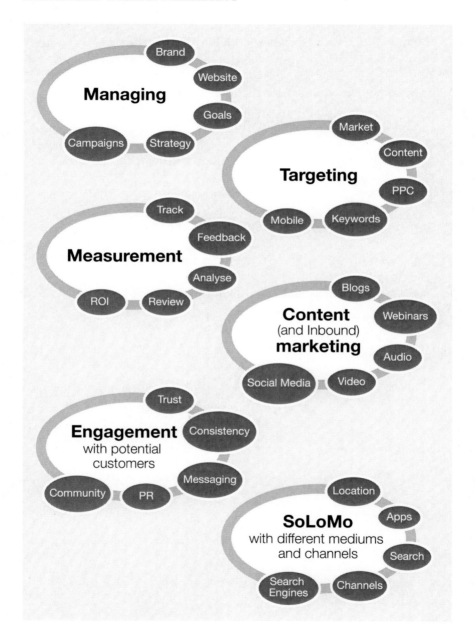

There are other areas that could be included in listing categories and activities as part of the digital marketing process. However, this type of illustration shows the many strands connecting important topics relevant to ensuring that you have an integrated marketing approach. Each goal needs looking at as well as the different actions relevant to the goal in order to give clarity and best practice. This will increase your chances of targeting the right companies or people in the right way.

KEY QUESTIONS

- How many channels are you using and how can you optimise them?
- How often do you review your inbound and content marketing?
- How well are you integrating your own digital marketing?

Chapter summary

Digital marketing is a powerful way of engaging with potential customers and showing them that you are aligned to their needs. To do this you need to engage with them and have the necessary marketing tools to support your goals, which then need to be communicated internally so that everyone is aware of them. This will help your marketing campaigns to be well managed. Goals can then become part of your digital marketing strategy. Also, make sure that everyone in a marketing role has bought into this to improve the chances of success.

The chapter also looked at setting up best practice principles, part of which is to set out a process internally to manage and measure your goals. This will help you develop a platform which will show your company, brand, products and services in their best light.

The last part of the chapter focused on different types of marketing channels and the importance of testing these to know which ones work the best. The type of channels you choose to communicate your marketing messages needs to be considered and the quality of the content you have on your website and its use in campaigns is a key part of this. Taking the time to get this right will give you the best chance of getting the ROI you were looking for.

Key points

✓ Set up a best practice set of principles to drive common marketing goals

✓ Ensure that your goals become part of a defined digital marketing strategy

✓ Take the time to research, discuss and deliver 'best practice'

✓ Create interesting, relevant and high-quality digital marketing content

✓ Test different channels to find out which ones work well

THREE
CHANGES THAT IMPACT ON THE CUSTOMER EXPERIENCE

CHAPTER TOPICS

- The impact of technology
- The customer experience
- Online purchasing and how it has changed behaviour

Introduction

This chapter looks at the impact of developments in digital technology that have changed customer expectations. This has made companies more aware of how to meet the challenges in marketing generally. It covers the need for a digital culture to be adopted in order for companies to keep up with the pace of change.

We will look at the efforts many companies have made in trying to fully understand the purchasing experience that buyers go through. It has led to improved communication in relation to the customer experience (CX). This has been greatly affected by digital media, which has resulted in changes being introduced to manage the 'customer journey' before, during and after a sale takes place.

The chapter looks at online purchasing in the B2C market and how consumers have changed and become more aware of products and services before they are purchased. This has meant that companies who sell to them have had to better understand their target audience and what drives buying decisions.

The impact of technology

The increased use of technology by companies in recent years has forced a change in the level of investment towards digital marketing. This has involved learning new ways to integrate marketing concepts into a company's culture.

However, Information Technology (IT) has played an important role in helping marketing departments (and agencies) understand and deliver digital campaigns. Responsive web design, data sharing, mobile devices and the speed of data transfer rates have helped to enhance people's digital experience.

The Web has meant that people in a marketing role have needed to embrace technology. It has also created a need for increased skill levels in this fast-moving process. Interaction with web developers, social media experts and data specialists are examples of how the impact of technology has allowed marketing departments to change. The same could apply to digital specialists who have had to adapt their knowledge to include marketing practices.

People and technology need to work together to communicate with potential customers and this involves dealing with a number of devices; PCs, laptops, tablets and mobile phones. It means IT, marketing departments and agencies need to think about building websites, how to handle data and run social media campaigns. Other areas to consider include communication, measurement and planning.

Communication

Whether you use a digital marketing agency or you have employed your own team, involve them in your marketing plans by having open communication. This should involve discussions in relation to Search Engine Optimisation (SEO), Pay Per Click (PPC) and social media. A marketing team will need to understand the brand value and revenue impact of different ways to spend a marketing budget, i.e. digital versus traditional marketing spend.

Measurement

Find common ground so that you have measurable outcomes to progress. This will help digital marketing campaign goals to be met. If no outcomes were agreed, it is hard to know how successful they actually were and the return on investment (ROI) becomes difficult to measure!

Plan

If you take the time to involve the key stakeholders in a digital marketing team, it will help any plan to be more successful. Listen to different points of view and agree next steps with time frames. Involve someone from your sales department where possible so that you get any follow-up sales activity and conversions factored in.

People in a marketing role are busy and planning is something that doesn't always result in people taking the time to meet each other – even if they work in the same building. If you need to discuss something with a colleague or marketing agency who works from a remote location, consider using business online conferencing as an alternative to an email or phone call. Take the time to do this because it helps to personalise communication and can lead to a more coordinated approach.

People, Process and Technology need to come together to form the successful delivery of your digital marketing. This can be achieved through elements that include well thought-out branding, good quality content in marketing campaigns and a responsive website design. This can be illustrated in the following way:

DIGITAL MARKETING INTEGRATION

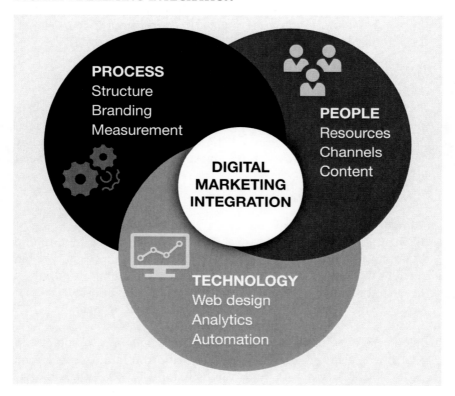

Bringing these elements together will help you combine the different strands needed to integrate your digital marketing process. In order to get stakeholders to work well together, define the purpose of any proposed work and get them to agree the method for this as well as outcomes. This will help people from different types of background understand the common goals and purpose of a marketing strategy.

Digital culture

Any change in transforming a marketing strategy to one which is primarily digital needs looking at introspectively. This in turn will require change and a marketing culture which is open to new ideas. It involves input and support from technical specialists who understand the world of social media and other digital platforms.

While technology has transformed digital marketing, there are other factors which need to be considered in order to maintain a potential customer's interest. Digital communication is still between people and future customers' needs should be at the forefront of any marketing strategy or campaign. It isn't enough to have a good product or rely on technology alone; questions like 'How does it fulfil a need?' and 'How can this be communicated?' need answering.

Technology can also alienate people: those who either don't understand it or don't feel at ease using it. Some digital marketing campaigns might not be successful if the target audience is one which doesn't primarily use social media as a method of receiving marketing communication (for example one consisting of over 65s). If this is the case, potential sales can be lost as a digital strategy to attract an audience with this demographic might not work.

That is why companies look at different categories of people (known as personas) when thinking about what type of marketing strategy to use. People can be split into age ranges in order to break down the categories for measurement. Surveys with this type of categorisation are regularly done to analyse the age ranges of people using social networks. This is useful for companies who have more users in the 25 – 34-year-old category compared with those over 65 years old, for example.

In order to understand a buyer, whether it is in a B2B or B2C market, companies have found that employing the right type and quality of people is a valuable way of getting the right culture. This has been linked with the type of business strategy and values the company has. Removing barriers internally helps people adapt to change and embrace it. A digital culture is a mixture of using technology to your advantage, managed by people who understand it in order to attract new customers.

Keeping up with the pace of change

Companies can find it hard to keep up with the pace of change in relation to digital technology. Many are aware of the importance of getting the right blend of digital interaction with their target audience; however, actually achieving this is not as easy. This is partly due to some competitors' business models changing. It means keeping up not only with digital technology but also how to compete in changing markets and changing business models.

This leads to a potentially challenging area for larger companies in that target markets and models to fit them are two completely separate strategic challenges. These could be looked at by different departments and this has the potential to slow down the process of finding a solution. That is why it is important for companies to understand the components which underpin this, for example:

- Looking at the real strengths you currently have in the market

- Understanding what threats exist, as well as where and who they come from

- Developing a marketing strategy that has digital technology at its core

- Experimenting with different digital marketing campaigns to find the right blend

- Making sure that your brand is seen as 'cutting edge', modern and relevant

This makes investing in the right areas easier to achieve. It will also involve listening to your customers. Change management is a topic in itself, which is important to embrace in order to keep up with the current state of a market. By doing so, you will be in a better position to meet the technological and cultural challenges ahead.

KEY QUESTIONS

- What changes in technology are taking place in your company that will affect digital marketing?

- How well are you equipped to deal with the challenges of a People, Process and Technology model?

- How would you describe your own digital culture and ability to adapt to change?

The customer experience

Putting the customer first

A company's values, as well as the products it sells, now play a larger role in the buying experience as a result of an increase in digital awareness and social media. This has meant that marketers have more pressure on them to achieve two key aspirations: to keep existing customers happy and to find new ones.

Customer interaction has become more complex as a company's ability to sell through a variety of media has increased, i.e. B2C – in a shop/store, mobile and online. Forms of communication via email or from a company's website have also added to the ways this can take place.

Customer surveys and satisfaction have become part of a company's review process into finding out what is and isn't working. It has made companies realise that the 'customer journey' is integrated into the process of someone purchasing products and services. Also, the increase in mobile phone usage globally is constantly changing the way people view information. This gives them the ability to buy 'on the go' rather than in person or on a computer.

The ability to view potential purchase information needs a different mindset from marketers. It involves being able to 'tap in' to what people want and what they don't want more quickly. People are better informed and better prepared now when it comes to the buying process.

Twenty years ago, in a B2B context, a buyer might want to know why and how a product or service could help them before engaging in a conversation about buying it. Now, that person will probably be very well aware of this and which companies sell what products, the prices they sell at and the value they offer. They will also be more knowledgeable about how strong the brand is and the real value that it offers their own company.

Sellers of B2B products and services may find that a sales cycle is shorter because of a buyer's preparation and that interaction with a potential supplier starts later in the process because of it. Companies are more aware in a digital era of how to access intelligence and information. The speed at which digital technology can be communicated has improved and this has helped customer understanding in relation to potential purchases.

Digital marketing has helped to reduce customer service costs as well as improve customer satisfaction levels. McKinsey found that consumers that used only digital channels were nearly 20 per cent more satisfied than those who purchased goods and services in other ways like call centres, (McKinsey, eCare customer survey).

With review websites, consumers can compare purchasing options and get real feedback from people who have bought items. While this is valuable to companies and marketers, it has the potential to damage them if care isn't taken to correct (and sometimes respond) to any poor reviews. That is why putting the customer first is a vital component of attracting and retaining them.

Changing expectations

Due to the continuing improvements in technology and the speed at which this is happening, companies need to adapt quickly. This can put pressure on marketing strategies which can easily become dated. Companies that do keep up to date with digital technology gain an advantage in the marketplace, which can help them stay ahead of their competitors.

Choice has become the norm for many people. If you can't supply something in a quick, easy and professional manner, there is likely to be a company that can.

Changes include affordable broadband in developing countries which is likely to increase dramatically the number of people who have access to the Internet. This means that for consumers in particular, the B2C market has the potential to keep growing at a high rate and, at the same time, there is likely to be an ever-changing set of demographics. This will force many companies to decide how best to separate and keep different types of target market aware of their products and services.

Changing expectations have helped to reinforce the number of ways companies can identify with their potential customers including listening more to what customers want, responding in real time and creating two-way conversations.

These changes have created a different type of language in marketing and have helped to make companies and their potential customers more aware of the existence of broader type of marketplace. This is evident in the rise of online purchasing and how it has changed consumer behaviour and the customer experience.

Customer engagement

Customer engagement is the interaction between potential buyers and sellers during the time the selling process takes place. With the progress of digital marketing there has been a much greater awareness and expectation from buyers in the B2B and B2C markets. This has led to companies looking at things more and more from a customer's perspective. You might say that this is fairly obvious and should have been done before the success of digital marketing, but it shows how companies have had to be more proactive than ever before in order to reach and maintain high customer service expectations.

Customers have become more choice-driven because the Web gave them more choices. Company buyers and consumers are able to look at a potential company's website and think about the brand and values that emanate from it. This has led to those in a marketing role having to rethink how to engage with their target audience.

Companies have realised that by understanding a customer's experience they can win more business and get a better ROI on their marketing campaigns. This is possible by defining their needs and linking this to the value of the products and services being sold. It sounds easy but, with the benefit of digital marketing, many companies have been able to reinvent themselves and adapt to a more informed way of selling.

There has been a stronger focus on the customer and a greater attempt to understand the actual experience they want when engaging with a potential supplier. This enables a company to align its products in a way which makes it easier for someone to have a good experience. Most purchases involve a 'buying cycle' which might include:

- Customer perception of a potential supplier

- Brand awareness (which can include your market, products, service)

- The buying process

- Interest in a product or solution

- Engagement with your company (and others)

- Decision-making capability

- Purchase

- After-sales service/account management

This can be illustrated in the follow way:

CUSTOMER BUYING CYCLE

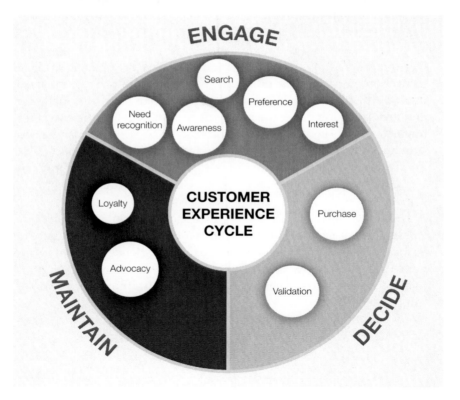

These stages can be categorised into three main *triggers* that determine the experience of a potential customer, the success of which will ultimately determine how long the engagement lasts.

1. Engage
When a potential customer begins to show interest due to an engagement with a website, social media, inbound marketing, a targeted campaign etc.

2. Decide
The point of decision-making leading to a purchase.

3. Maintain
When customer loyalty leads to them being an advocate of the product or service.

Customer loyalty is tested over time with new products and those from competitors. Buyers often go through a review process to establish whether to maintain loyalty to a particular brand. By defining and then breaking down the components which define the customer buying cycle, it is much easier to focus on each one. This enables companies to establish how well aligned they are in each particular area. From this, any planning of a digital marketing campaign can be formed and specific areas can be reviewed and measured.

A customer's experience can differ depending on how they buy something, for example via the Web, a mobile app, on the telephone or face to face. By segmenting the type of experience, marketers are better placed to know how to deal with it. With social media platforms, customers have almost instant access to information which can reinforce or undermine a company's reputation. This has forced many companies to rethink their sales and marketing strategies to align themselves with 'best practice' customer needs.

So, what can companies do to try and ensure a positive customer experience? In order to match someone's needs and fulfil them they need to:

- Listen to their customers

- Focus on the value being offered

- Articulate USPs

- Be positive, professional and helpful

- Communicate in a personal way

- Try and make an emotional connection

- Be responsive

You'll notice than none of these areas are automated, they are personal. Once you know what your customer's experience is, categorise it. This will enable you to have different mini strategies for each segment. For example, you might divide them into ones where customers actually promote your products, are neutral about them or still haven't become advocates. Customer surveys like the Net Promoter Score® (NPS) have enabled companies to define and measure customer loyalty. This has helped to define an easy-to-understand categorisation process.

The benefits of a good customer experience should be obvious: to reach a much larger potential audience leading to increased sales potential. This is why something which, for many years, didn't have a strong focus for some companies, is now considered to be a top priority.

The power of customer feedback

Customer feedback is important. In order to engage with your target audience you should set up alerts for your brand(s). Being able to respond to people in real time, especially a complaint, can improve customer satisfaction ratings and loyalty. You need to monitor social media platforms and respond as quickly as possible. Make sure that you do this for all those you are communicating on.

Happy customers are more likely to tell someone else about their experience as well as becoming an advocate for your products or services. With an enquiry or a complaint, make sure that you prioritise on the quality of your response rather than on a quick response. Look at setting up a bespoke customer support account on social media channels. This will again help to show that you want to help people who have genuine after-sales complaints. Get used to relying on user feedback and data analytics as a way of maintaining best practice customer service.

Customer service

As social media networks have forced companies to adapt, so has the way in which they serve customers. In many examples, face-to-face or telephone conversations have often been replaced online with interactive digital conversations. The impact on customer service has improved in relation to digital marketing and social media. It has become more important for companies to have a good after-sales service either with online and/or customer-facing channels.

In some ways social media networks have become a type of customer service channel, allowing discussion and much information to be communicated. This applies not only to buyers but also to many other people who read comments and blogs. In order to better prepare yourself for this type of customer service interaction, you should prepare how to deal with this, for example:

- Drive a customer service culture

- Align your customer service with your business objectives

- Be aware of what your customers buy

- Think of how you can keep your customer service up to a high standard

Even if someone isn't directly in a customer-facing role, they still need to understand and demonstrate a customer service ethic. This starts at the top of a company's infrastructure and should be part of any overall business strategy.

KEY QUESTIONS

- Why type of customer experience programme does you have in place?
- How do you track customer feedback?
- How well equipped are you to offer great customer service?

Online purchasing and how it has changed behaviour

Shopping online is a form of electronic commerce (e-commerce). This concept began in 1979 and, by 1991, the Web made it possible for companies to trade online (Amazon began doing this in 1995). The shopping experience may be different from traditional shopping, but there are a number of areas which have helped consumers have confidence in it, for example:

- Buying products is easy and quick

- There is a greater amount of choice

- Most suppliers allow returns if you are not satisfied with the goods you received (providing you haven't used them)

- Online shopping outlets like Amazon provide feedback from other customers

- There are trusted online payment providers, e.g. PayPal

This method of shopping is very convenient for many consumers because of these factors and it gives them flexibility. The growth of the Web has changed the way many customers buy products and services. Before this, consumers might look to friends for referrals, a business telephone directory, read something from a catalogue or visit a shop/store in person. They would go through some type of process to raise their awareness of a product before considering a purchase.

Other factors like loyalty programmes and the increased speed of people's decision-making have raised customer awareness to a higher level. People often feel confident about buying online rather than having to visit a shop in person as information is easy to access on a company's website.

Online retail sales are forecast to grow by over 12% over the next five years from the end of 2016 in Western Europe to reach €378 billion (internetretailing.net from a Forrester Data report). This has been put down to increased levels of cost effectiveness and convenience for online shoppers helping companies to improve the customer experience.

The increase in online shopping has put pressure on traditional methods of shopping and the trend looks set to continue. It is forcing major chains to rethink how they market their products and how digital marketing can continue to help with this process. It has also made them more aware of how to sell online.

Traditional retailers adapting to change

The growth of online shopping has put pressure on retailers to adapt. Many have had to invest significantly more in online shopping to help increase sales. It has given consumers much more choice about how they shop and has improved the shopping experience. It has changed the way they think which, in turn, has affected the way they buy. So, what type of factors affect someone's buying decisions? They can be categorised by defining internal and external factors.

External factors include areas like economic or social situations, which will be affected by:

- The economy

- Culture

- Social class

- Role in the family

- Technological change

- Political change

Internal factors include individual values, which could be affected by someone's:

- Beliefs and attitudes

- Lifestyle

- Occupation and income

- Character and motivation

- Perception of needs

- Age and education

This can be summarised and illustrated in the following way.

CONSUMER BEHAVIOUR

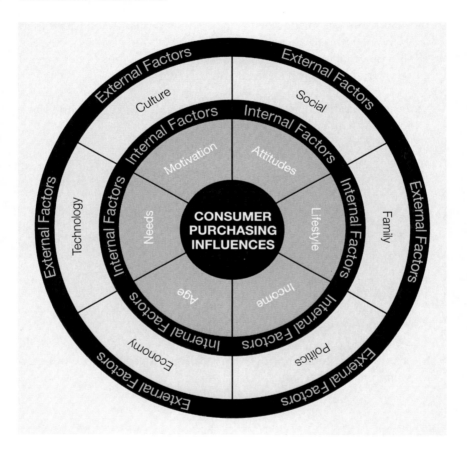

Companies have had to adapt to customer purchasing behaviour both in B2B and B2C markets and better understand the personas of their target audience. This has required research so that the right type of digital marketing is applied to maximise the sales potential. Marketers have become much more aware of the people who buy their brands and which digital marketing channels to use in order to promote them.

People now have greater choice to look at different suppliers and brands and make comparisons between products and services. This has led to a reduction in the time it takes to make a decision about a purchase. One of the ways that consumers have been able to make more informed decisions is through price comparison websites. They have also been able to access data to enable them to compare prices, quality and the delivery of service.

KEY QUESTIONS

- How has the growth in online purchasing affected you?
- How have you adapted to changes in B2B and B2C buyer behaviour?

Chapter summary

Digital marketing has changed the way that companies interact and engage with potential and existing customers. It is now about communicating with your target audience in a relevant way to build longer term and sustainable relationships when promoting a brand.

The impact of change in a digital world has forced companies to rethink how they approach the balance between technology and people in relation to marketing. This has involved an introspective look in order to manage the culture as well as the resources it needs. While digital marketing strategies need to be at the core of this process, so do the people in an organisation.

This has led companies to improve the customer experience. Winning new customers can be transient; understanding them, meeting their needs and retaining them is harder. Companies that have embraced change have increased their market share.

Finally, the increase in online purchasing by consumers has put pressure on companies to deliver a more flexible purchasing platform. By doing so, marketers have been able to target people by knowing more about them. This involves a better understanding of the types of products and services that they want to buy and making it easier for companies to do business with them.

Key points

✓ Take the time to understand how changes in technology can help digital marketing

✓ Think about the strength of your relationships and the customer experience

✓ Look at a customer's buying cycle and how you can align your marketing to it

✓ Learn from the feedback you get from your customers

✓ If you sell online, get a good understanding of consumer behaviour

FOUR
GETTING YOUR WEBSITE TO ADD VALUE

Introduction

This chapter will look at what makes a good website and how it can support your digital marketing. A good user experience (UX) with a computer interface can make it easier for the people reading your website to really engage with your company and the products and services you sell. It can help to promote your vision and become an integral part of building a future business relationship with your target audience. We will look at the elements you should have on your website and the need to make it easy to navigate and explore.

The chapter will look at how to use a website to support your digital marketing, what to put in it and what to leave out. We will look at how it can support digital marketing and what you can do to improve its performance. Finally, we will look at ways in which you can make your own website more interactive. This will help improve its optimisation in order to try and differentiate your value proposition.

What makes a good website?

Nearly every company of SME size and above, selling a product or service, will have a website. What type of content you choose depends on what you are selling and how much thought you have put in to make it effective. People look at a company's website for a number of reasons. These include its products and services and a potential supplier's expertise and values.

A good website helps a company to differentiate itself and to reinforce its brand(s). Much depends on what a website is actually designed for. One which sells online will be different from one which looks to inform. Many websites are built using a responsive design so that the content can be easily viewed whether from a desktop, laptop, tablet or mobile phone. What content to include can be subjective but there are certain features that need to be included.

An example of how a website can function can be seen in the following illustration:

FEATURES OF A GOOD WEBSITE

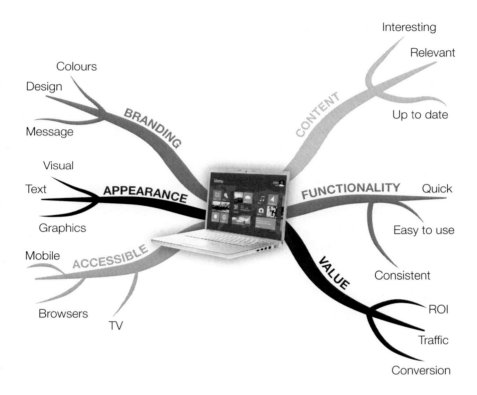

Deciding on its purpose

Before you start to either build or change your website, first look at what it is designed to do and in what order, for example:

- Inform

- Promote your company/advertise

- Promote your products or services

- Promote your experience and history

- Promote your brand(s)

- Sell online

- Communicate with potential customers

- Provide regular blogs

- Support your customers

Other questions that people in a marketing role should consider asking in relation to a websites structure and content include:

- Who is the intended audience?

- What content do you want in it?

- How do you intend to get people to it?

- How easy is it going to be to navigate?

- What are its differentiators (compared with competitors)?

- What value does it offer?

- Most importantly – what do you want people to do once they access it?

It is a good idea to get feedback from users of your website even if you have been trading for many years, especially if you are looking to change it. This will allow you to see things from someone else's point of view. Another key point that is often lost on marketers is not to focus on the *features* of your products and services alone. You need to explain very simply but clearly *how* they work and what the *value* is to the target audience. Some websites do the first two elements well but don't always clearly define the value to the recipient, which is the most important element.

This sounds obvious but if you are over-focused on promoting your brand(s), it can come across to someone as all about you! What is needed is a balance between what you sell and how you sell it, with the benefits. By doing this you have a better chance of engaging with people in a positive way and coming across as focusing on their needs.

Website content

Think about what content you want to put in, whether you are building a website for the first time or are upgrading your existing one (this is covered in *Chapter 2, Creating a digital marketing strategy* in the content marketing section). Look at what the goals are for the content on your website and each page. Decide on how well they link together and how strong the messages are.

Keep your content fresh and up to date. Some websites have out-of-date information and blogs that were written many weeks before. This takes time to do but you want to give a positive impression that you take the updating of information on your own website seriously. If you use Facebook, Twitter or LinkedIn, join or start relevant discussions with the view to adding some knowledge, experience and value on a topic rather than to promote your own agenda. This will add more value to your target audience.

Make it easy for someone to contact you either by email or phone (if that is what your business model requires). Most B2B companies will give locations of offices to either inform a user generally or to show where an office can be visited. A user is likely to stay on a website longer if the site is easy to navigate and the content is relevant and engaging.

Think about the words used and how well your written messages actually read to you and to others and take care in relation to supporting images, videos etc. Presenting an image, an idea or information is a skill, especially when you need them to look simple in their design and be easily communicated.

Navigation

It is important to think about the hierarchy you use on your website in order to make navigation as easy as possible. This applies regardless of the device people are looking at, for example a desktop or a mobile phone.

Try not to have too many tabs or buttons and use header names which are simple and easy to remember, but think carefully about which words you use so that you differentiate yourself from other competitors in your market. Choosing the right keywords is also a factor for Search Engine Optimisation (SEO). Other ideas to help you get the best out of the navigation process include:

- Don't put too many items in a menu list

- Be careful of using drop down menus – it can encourage users to miss important items and this can be difficult on mobile devices

- Use a simple layout to make it easy for users to follow (unless your branding requires a more complex design)

- Put in 'calls to action' to encourage users to carry out certain activities, e.g. to contact you, sign up to a newsletter

- Think carefully about the structure of your menus – put yourself in the user's position trying to find something on your website

- Let users know where they are on a particular page to keep them engaged – using 'breadcrumb navigation' can help with this*

---

*Breadcrumb navigation uses a hierarchy so that users can navigate more easily on a website and reduce the number of steps taken and keep track of their locations.

Making a site easy to navigate is imperative and worth taking the time to do. This will help people move from page to page easily and in a way which encourages them to complete the actions you want them to. Also think about the clarity of the navigation process and how easy it is to do.

Optimisation

Much of how optimised a website is will depend on how it is written, technically and contextually. This is particularly important when planning how to get the best out of your SEO. Areas which affect website optimisation include:

- Headings

- Sub-headings

- Underlying optimise code, i.e. clean HTML

- Making it easily shareable on social media websites

Onsite content which links to other words or phrases and is preferably unique should be used. This includes targeted key words used to promote your products or services.

Optimisation and SEO are closely linked and are primarily about ensuring that users find the content they are looking for easily and quickly. That is why the structure and content of a website need to be thought out in a way which makes navigation and optimisation easy. As part of the optimisation process, think about what your key words are for the website generally and particularly for each page. You need to check how long a page takes to load from different devices in order to ensure that your site has optimum responses to this.

Optimisation is about the speed at which someone can gain access to a website or page and to rank this in terms of a Google-type search. This has been helped in recent years by the introduction of faster Internet speeds globally which has made it easier for websites to get repeat visits. These are key drivers which companies will want to take advantage of and which are worth investing the time in to get right.

KEY QUESTIONS

- What makes your website different from others selling similar products and services?
- How often do you review your competitors' websites?
- Why would someone visit your website over your competitors?

How a website supports digital marketing

For most companies, a website is a place for potential customers to view or make enquiries before buying products and services. For others it is a chance to buy something online. For other companies in the B2B market, a website can be the chance to engage and develop a business relationship with its target audience.

This means that you often need to use it as a support mechanism for a wider strategy to promote digital marketing. Investment of time and effort in digital marketing can increase the number of leads you get as well as sales. Use of SEO and PPC can also improve the rankings of your website in a Google search (this is covered in *Chapter 6, Getting the best out of data analytics*).

Many small companies with five employees or fewer don't have a website. The main reason for this is that they don't believe it will help them achieve growth (Redshift Research). Ironically, statistics show that having a website can improve the chances of a company growing. Another survey in the USA showed that 97 per cent of small businesses said that they would recommend having a website (Verisign). The reasons for this were cited as:

- Helping them to promote their products and services

- Building credibility

- Making it easier to get more customers

- Achieve growth faster

- Gain a competitive advantage

This is highly relevant to the discussion about how a website can support digital marketing as these points help to demonstrate the value that having one offers. This can be illustrated in the following way, which shows how improvement in Web performance can have a 'knock-on effect' and lead to more business.

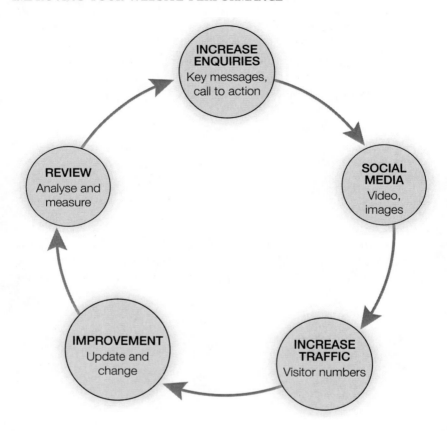

Having a website allows companies to have a presence and be viewed by potential buyers. It can give credibility to the products and services on offer and an insight into the history of the company, its skills and experience. To build on this, marketers use a website as a 'shop window' for self-promotion. Having one makes a company accessible and creates a positive environment for viewers of it.

In supporting digital marketing, a website can be viewed 24 hours a day, 7 days a week. This gives potential buyers a choice as to when they view it and if sales can be achieved directly from it, an ability to trade which is not restricted by office hours.

For small and medium-sized enterprises (SMEs), it is also a chance for promotion at a local level. Customers don't always buy from large companies alone and a website can help a smaller company show its worth and value. It can also mean that potential buyers worry less about the size of a supplier and more about its ability to meet their needs at the right price.

What to put in and what to leave out!

Website design and content differs and it is a challenge to get the balance right in terms of showing too much or too little, but there are a number of basic recommendations that any company should look at and implement, regardless of its size.

1. Use language that people can understand. This will help to make it easier to understand your core messages and explanations of how you help solve particular challenges and fulfil a potential customer's needs.

2. Try and enter into a dialogue with your customers; this will help to engage them and improve the chances of customer loyalty. Think about the customer service element of what you are selling. For example, does your website content include after-sales contact information and details?

3. If you do sell online, make it easy for buyers. Try it out yourself or get feedback from others as to how they found the experience. If someone doesn't find it easy to use, they will most likely choose another supplier so this is worth getting right!

Think about any information you might need to put on your website which can answer any potential questions that a customer might have either before or after a sale. A Frequently Answered Questions (FAQs) page can resolve this. This can act as a good way of pre-handling potential objections that can affect a customer's confidence in your products and services. It also looks professional and can genuinely help a potential customer to understand elements that relate to their purchasing requirements.

Ways that you can make your website more interactive

Every company would like to maximise the amount of leads and new business opportunities it gets from its website. In order to do this, there are a number of relatively easy actions that you can take in order to increase the number of visitors to your site. This can be done without relying on SEO or PPC to do this for you, for example:

- Read and follow the Google Webmaster guidelines (support. google.com/webmasters)

- Look at how often you update and review your website

- Read some of your own blogs

- Check web pages and try and look at them from a new user's point of view

- Think about the graphics you use

- Compare your site with those of your competitors

These types of suggestions might seem obvious but if you aren't doing any or all of them you might not be getting the amount of website traffic you could. You can look to add more 'long-tail variations' to your web pages; these are keywords which you can include in the text and which can convert at a higher rate with Google, for example this will help to bring you higher up the list in a Google search engine.

When you write titles and descriptions, think about the words you use carefully as this will determine how your pages appear in search results. Describe your area of expertise and what unique selling points (USPs) you have and why a potential customer should buy from you.

You can link a website page to another which has a high authority on your domain and this can help the target page to rank better. You should make a list of the highest value pages you'd like to improve a ranking on and identify the pages which have the highest priority. As a website's homepage is most likely to be the most important page on a domain, it is probably the best one to choose for an authority page to link from. Other ways in which you can increase traffic include:

- Host webinars

- Speak at conferences to increase your exposure

- Put some video content on your website

- Get more active on social media and use it to promote your content

- Leave interesting and relevant comments on other websites

- Make sure your site is fast

- Invite others to blog on your site

- Mix up the type and size of your content

- Advertise

You can write content that encourages other sites to link to yours. This referral traffic will again help improve your potential for new enquiries. You can also create a site map which will make it easier for visitors to navigate it. Here is a quick summary of four main actions you can take:

- *Refresh* your content

- *Give* something away

- *Post* information online

- *Share* content

This can be illustrated with actions you can list in each of the areas, for example:

MAKING THE MOST OUT OF YOUR WEBSITE

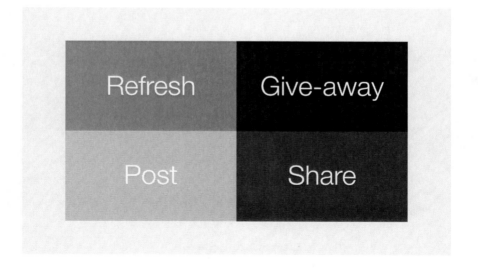

Refresh

Keep your content fresh by writing new information, for example blogs, on a regular basis. Look at how you can grab someone's attention and make sure the information is easy to read.

Give away

Think about what you can give away free that will entice someone to want to come back and engage with your products or services. This could include:

- All or part of an e-book

- A design template

- A report

- A tutorial

- A video

Use a Creative Commons licence to make it clear what users and can't do with your material.

Post

Think about information you can use to post online which can entice people. This could be a blog or a newsletter, something which engages your target audience. It might come with an offer of signing up to a regular newsletter or a give-away item.

Share

Look at sharing social media links; you can use Twitter, Facebook or Instagram to share links to your content. A list of tips and advice to help people in your market is another idea which can draw people to your website. Once there, you may find that other pages are looked at which will improve your profile.

Updating information and thinking of new ideas to keep a website interesting takes time and effort. Getting feedback will also help you get a different perspective on your website's value, but doing this will help you to attract more traffic and increase the chances of potential enquiries.

KEY QUESTIONS

- How often do you read your own website pages and material?
- What free content do you post, give away and share?

Chapter summary

A website is relatively easy to create and maintain. However, making it relevant, interesting and differentiating it from your competitors isn't. This is why you need to take the time to think about what it says, what it does and the values it is trying to convey. Good navigation of a website makes it easier for your target audience to interact with your company. The information you put in it will help support the marketing messages you want to send. That is often why a decision to leave something out is as important as what to leave in.

Part of this decision will come from the content you have put on your website and which words and phrases you want to use. You also need to think about many of the actions you can take which will help you improve the quality of the engagement with your target audience. This doesn't have to involve a high level of investment; it is more about a focus on attention to detail and the regularity of contact with the people you want to engage with. This includes the types of information you want to show and share with them.

You should think about ways in which you can make your site interactive in order to get more 'hits'. This will make it stand out, give credibility to your marketing messages and make it easier for potential customers to engage with your company.

Key points

✓ Look at the structure of your website for marketing purposes

✓ Think about how your website will support other areas of digital marketing

✓ Decide what to leave in and leave out of your website

✓ Think about ways in which you can constantly engage with your target audience

FIVE
PLATFORMS FOR DIGITAL MARKETING COMMUNICATION

CHAPTER TOPICS

- Social media networks:
  - Facebook
  - Twitter
  - YouTube
  - LinkedIn
  - Instagram
  - Pinterest
- Creating a social media strategy

Introduction

Digital communication on social media websites has helped to revolutionise the marketing process. This chapter focuses on the value to companies in making the most out of using social media. It will look at some of the most popular social media networks, which are attractive to marketers due to the vast amount of information shared by users and the potential for advertising on them.

Many sites have become successful platforms by influencing buyers/ consumers in B2B and particularly B2C markets. Their ability to provide a way for people to communicate online has forced companies to rethink their digital marketing strategies. This chapter focuses on the type of audience that some of the most popular social media networks are looking for. This can then help marketers to continue to think of ways of using this as part of their own target marketing.

We will look at the importance of creating a separate strategy for social media. This needs to be part of an overall digital marketing strategy. We will look at the stages you should follow in order to get the best return on your investment (ROI). The chapter will also look at the impact social media has on consumers so that marketers can define different strategies for different types of demographics.

Social media networks

The appeal of social media can be explained by people's desire to communicate with others, entertain and be entertained. This has resulted in users participating in social and business discussions and following people's thoughts and opinions socially on a regular basis. Users can write something (e.g. posts on Facebook or 'tweets' on Twitter) or upload images that can be shared (e.g. on Instagram or Pinterest).

Communication between social media site users has given digital marketers the chance to engage with users in a different way from traditional marketing in order to promote their brand(s). Many companies targeting this market realised that engaging in a conversation or advertising was a successful way of getting user engagement.

With advertising opportunities on social media sites like Facebook and Twitter, digital marketers have seen a change in the way marketing budgets have been spent in recent years. This has led to a split in the percentage of spend compared to traditional forms of marketing (see *Chapter 7, Integrating with traditional forms of marketing*).

The growth of social media since 2010 has been staggering. In 2016 there were over 3 billion active global Internet users – nearly half the world's population. Around 2.3 billion of these used social media.

GROWTH IN SOCIAL MEDIA PLATFORMS

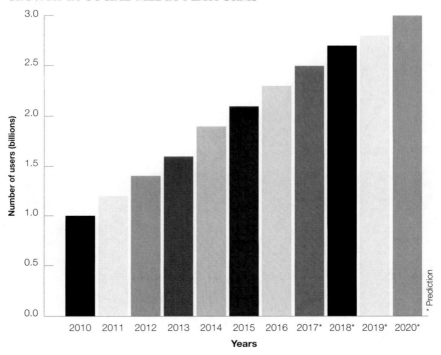

(Information from a combination of public domain related websites including pewinternet.org, smartinsights.com and emarketer.com)

Social media has given companies an opportunity to better understand their target audience by monitoring responses and comments made by users. Campaigns can be segmented to see which works best and information about customer buying patterns and behaviour can be more easily identified and tracked.

What makes social media influential and relevant is partly dependent on which network you want to use to promote your products and services. Each one works in a different way and is looking to attract a certain type of target audience. As most social media sites are not primarily focused on business, you need to think carefully about your focus.

There are now many social media sites and in order to get a better understanding of them we will look at six. However, the first two are primarily used for *business* purposes (LinkedIn and Twitter). The next four are primarily used for *social* purposes (Facebook, YouTube, Pinterest and Instagram). All of these have potential for advertising, which is of great interest to digital marketers. The following chart shows the 2016 global usage for our chosen social media platforms.

SOCIAL MEDIA USERS

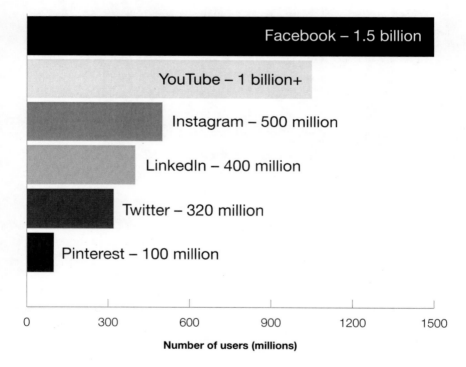

Number of users (millions)

(smartinsights.com, brandwatch.com and social media websites)

Let us now look at six of the main social media networks and how they can be utilised for marketing purposes.

Linked in

LinkedIn is a business social networking site launched in 2003. It allows users to communicate with other professionals. A member's profile page can include their employment history, education and their professional contact network. It has a basic and premium membership, the former of which is free. With the basic you can only have full contact with people that you already have some type of business association or relationship with.

The premium membership is a subscription service which allows users to gain access to LinkedIn's database and provides better targeting of new contacts for business purposes. Bought by Microsoft in 2016 it has over 460 million users in 200 countries (statista.com); however, only about 25 per cent of people use it on a monthly basis. Its site has been translated into 24 different languages.

LinkedIn advertising provides marketers with a way of communicating with people in business-related roles. It allows them to target users by industry, company, skill set, job title and group (if someone belongs to one). You can configure your advertisement (ad) and see how large your target audience is, for example how many people work in insurance in a particular country or globally. You can use this information even if you are not currently going to target that market in relation to advertising.

Its advertising engine may not be as good as that of Facebook or Google but it is functional. You can put multiple people on an account and collaborate on ads, including the ability to create multiple versions of ads in one campaign. There is also a dashboard to monitor ad performance and a button to turn ad campaigns on and off.

There are some challenges with LinkedIn. For example, its click through rate isn't that high – Facebook and Twitter do much better; the cost of running ad campaigns can be relatively high; users can receive a large number of spam (unsolicited or junk) mails, which can be frustrating; it takes time to set up conversations at the beginning of a targeted campaign; and its primary function is as a business network where users can resent the potential intrusion of advertising and therefore advertisers!

However, LinkedIn is very good for business exposure which can lead to an increase in your web traffic to blogs and to your website. It's a good way for people to stay up to date with what's happening in a particular industry and with individuals that you might be targeting. It also gives people in a B2B context, who represent a company, the opportunity to promote their own skills and the brand of the company they work for.

Twitter aims to provide social networking via short messages, a maximum of 140 characters, called tweets. It is designed for both companies and individuals and, once you register, you can read and post tweets (if you aren't registered, then you can only read them). Launched in 2006, the service currently has around 320 million active users.

Its main competitor is probably Tumblr which can be used for texts, pictures, video and audio communication. Tumblr differs from Twitter in that it is more of a blogging site and there is no limit to the amount of text a user can post.

You can advertise on Twitter and, to do so, you will need to select your campaign objectives. In order to get the most out of a campaign, you can use specific messages to promote a product or service directly. You can grow followers with promoted accounts and you can also increase your potential leads with lead generation cards. These are tweets that allow companies to collect names and emails directly on Twitter.

Twitter can be a cost-effective way of engaging with potential customers for digital marketing purposes. There is no charge to open a Twitter account and you can target potential customers in a B2B or B2C market by choosing to 'follow' them. This helps to build up a network that can give you leads and future sales. Twitter allows you to send messages at any time, which can give opportunities to send out important tweets before your competitors might.

For business purposes, Twitter offers some fundamental digital marketing benefits. These include:

- Promoting your brand

- Researching trends in the market

- Helping to promote two-way communication

- Helping with lead generation

- Getting valuable feedback

- Following current trends

If there are challenges using Twitter it is because there is no visual content, it is difficult to go into detail about a particular topic with only a limited number of characters and it has limited advertising benefits. It also has relatively high spam content and it can be time consuming to keep tweets up to date.

However, it is a popular and useful digital marketing tool that provides quick and easy communication to a targeted audience – a tweet goes to everyone who is following you; it is easy to use; and with its character limitation, it ensures that you avoid sending and receiving overly long messages.

facebook

Formed in 2004, Facebook is the largest online social network and it is used to upload and share content with 'friends' (people you choose). With 2 billion users, it does have huge business potential: a company can target a particular type of user and have direct communication with potential customers.

Facebook allows you to find your target audience and this is a powerful way to drive traffic to your website. It can help give your company increased exposure to potential new customers, it doesn't cost anything to create a page and it can give companies a better SEO return than investing in some other social networks. It also gives you a way of looking at what your competitors are doing! As Facebook is primarily a social networking site, getting the most value out of it for business purposes can be a challenge. However, there are some actions you can take in order to maximise your chances.

Look at ways in which you can communicate with your audience

A common mistake can be to promote your products and services by using Facebook as an advertising board. However, to get the best out of it you should look to focus on the people you are communicating with. This will help to engage them in the challenges they face and the needs they might have in relation to the solutions you offer, but not the products or services directly. By doing this you will come across as objective, helpful and relevant.

Look at ways in which you can use Facebook's news feed advertisements

You need to link any ad you promote to a Facebook page if you want to add it to the news feed as this can help you promote your products and services. Of course, you want the readers of an ad to like your page. This is a way of promoting your brand that offers a chance to engage with your target audience and to get your main marketing objectives across.

Get reviews and testimonials

Facebook allows companies to get feedback from potential B2B company individuals as well as consumers. It gives them a chance to review your products and services, which can act as a powerful reference for potential new customers who might use this endorsement to influence their own buying decisions.

Share opinions about your own market

You can get involved in discussions about challenges and changes in your own market and within your own company by writing and commenting on blogs. This can enhance your credibility and improve other Facebook users' knowledge about your company and you as a business professional.

Improve the results you get for SEO and PPC

Although your company may not initially rank near the top as a business name, by having a Facebook page you will help to promote it. This is particularly useful for new and lesser-known companies who want to use the Facebook brand to promote themselves.

There are some areas when using Facebook that you need to be mindful of when you look to engage with other users or advertise your products and services, for example:

- It is hard to engage with someone who doesn't comment or 'like' something

- There can be a high amount of spam

- Business groups are hard to create

- All of your posts are made public

- When you advertise, conversion rates are not always high

- Advertising is based on bid mechanisms (so ads can be outbid)

- It can be hard to know if a profile you are targeting is real or fake

Structuring a campaign can sometimes be challenging because the criteria used for a search can be interpreted in an ambiguous way. However, it is a good way to drive online sales as it is affordable and relationships are relatively easy to build. You can be tagged in posts by brand ambassadors and you have the ability to promote specific products.

Ad targeting is very specific and results are easy to measure. Any form of media can be used on Facebook for business and you can split marketing campaigns to find out what does and doesn't work. You can also stop marketing on Facebook at any time.

Facebook has a place for those companies wanting to use it as a digital marketing platform. With over 500 million active users (half of which log on daily), Facebook can be a powerful way of getting involved in a global community. It states that it shares more than 30 billion pieces of content every month, which is why companies use it to help promote their brand in a subtle, positive way through referrals, discussions and customer feedback.

YouTube was created in 2005 and enables users to upload videos which can be viewed, shared, commented on and rated. It has over a billion users per month worldwide and reaches more 18 to 34 year-olds in the USA than any other social media network (Top Online Video Sites in the US, nielsen.com).

Bought by Google in 2006, most of its content is uploaded by individuals rather than companies. As the world's largest video sharing site, YouTube can be used to promote products and services. Using a search for names, keywords, products etc., videos can help someone find a relevant social or business interest.

Companies can use YouTube to look at what competitors are doing in relation to selling as well as to understand the best way to position their own brands. There are a number of distinct advantages in having a YouTube account, for example:

- Reach – it has a large audience

- You can advertise (and there is no charge for the first five seconds of an ad)

- You can measure your website traffic

- Advertising can be very cost-effective

- The length of a video isn't capped

- You can place links on a video to act as a natural backlink (i.e. to your website)

There are some factors that can affect its marketing potential in relation to advertising spend, for example:

- It doesn't allow for customisation (when tagging locations, for example)

- You can't control the type of video your ad will be shown with

- Different branding may confuse your target audience

- Negative reviews can damage your brand's reputation

- A good video doesn't guarantee a high number of viewings

- Online video campaigns don't always reach the target audience

- Showing customer and product support information

YouTube can be an effective way to promote and support a product as well as being a valuable communication tool. Compared with television, advertising can be very cost-effective. Its analytics can help to assess the true measurement of who is watching a video and when, which helps in the measurement of marketing spend. Also, video viewings are increasing which means higher number of potential customers being targeted.

There are other social media sites on which you can advertise. However, the focus will be on just two because of the nature of their target audience.

Instagram

Instagram is a photo sharing app that was created in 2010. Facebook acquired it in 2012 and, by the end of 2015, it had over 500 million users (business.instagram.com). It only uses photo images and video, up to 15 seconds, which users can edit. It is primarily a mobile app; you can advertise on it and it is easy to use. Instagram is visual and some of its selling points in relation to digital marketing includes:

- It allows companies to advertise

- The number of users is very attractive to advertisers

- It has a distinct target market – primarily 25 to 34 year-olds

- Sharing photos allows users to connect with each other

- It allows companies to promote brands to a relatively new target audience

- Content can be shared on other social media networks

What differentiates it (and sites like Pinterest) from other sites is its focus on photos rather than text, something which can encourage an emotional connection with users which helps drive traffic to it.

In terms of the challenges it presents to digital marketers, there is no separation between business and social accounts and it has limited functionality on desktop/laptop PCs as you can't save photos on these. Also, as its target audience is geared towards a younger generation, marketers need to think about the age range of potential customers for their brand(s). However, the social aspect of Instagram is something which advertisers find attractive and this makes it a worthwhile target for many marketers.

Founded in 2010, Pinterest is a mobile and social media network which offers photo sharing and has around 100 million users. You can upload and manage photos, called 'pins', and look at other users' photos. It isn't a social network in the same way that Facebook is. Like Instagram, most users fall in the 25 to 34 year-old age group and as many as 80 per cent of its users are female. For digital marketers, there are a number of benefits in engaging with it:

- It allows advertisers to reach a large target audience

- Photo messages can be a very powerful form of advertising

- It drives a lot of traffic

- It has a high amount of user engagement

- It integrates with a Facebook and Twitter account

Advertisers can create a business account and Pinterest is good to drive SEO because it is regularly indexed by search engines, i.e. where data is collected and stored for later retrieval.

However, Pinterest is limited in that there can be potential copyright issues if you 'pin' images owned by others; it isn't primarily business-orientated; and content isn't always shared and can go to places that you can't control. However, Pinterest can help companies reinforce their brand by increasing their visibility. It is easy to use, generates referral traffic and its content is ideal for visual exposure. Also, if your business targets are women, it is a good way to reach this audience.

There are many other social networks that have not been included here, for example:

- **Tumblr** – microblogging and sharing of videos, audio and quotes

- **Google+** – social network that works off a Google account

- **Reddit** – entertainment social network

- **Flikr** – image and video hosting

This shows the different types of communication that people are involved with on a global basis. Social media networks earned over $30 billion from advertising in 2016 (statista.com). This brings sharply into focus the huge faith that companies investing in digital marketing advertising have in social media as a potential channel for earnings.

KEY QUESTIONS

- How well do you know different social media platforms?
- Which social media platforms do you engage with?
- What type of target audience are you trying to communicate with?

Creating a social media strategy

In order to ensure that you get a healthy ROI from an engagement with social media networks, you should create a social media strategy. This needs to be part of an overall digital marketing strategy, covered in *Chapter 2, Creating a digital marketing strategy*. This will help you to set a benchmark in terms of expectations as well as a list of rules to be used as part of the process.

The strategy should define common marketing objectives in relation to social media networks including elements like targeting and tools to measure the success of campaigns. This will help to reduce any risks attached to a campaign as well as give you something to refer back to. You should devise a process so that you can compare the stages you go through. This can be illustrated in the following way:

STAGES OF A SOCIAL MEDIA STRATEGY

Goals	Preparation	Execution	Monitor	Review
Sales revenue	Content	Differentiate	Measurement/ analytics	Measurement
Website traffic	Choose platforms	Build brand	Retention	Feedback
Channels	Timing	Blogs/video views	Customer service	Brand awareness
Brand/vision	Roadmap	Timeframe	Competitors	Adjustment
Establish budget	Investment	Support	Campaign management	ROI

For a social media strategy to be successful, everyone involved in its planning and implementation should understand what is needed.

This involves a clear understanding of what your brand values are and who you are targeting. With larger companies, ensure that marketing a particular brand on social media complements other products and services you might sell and is consistent with the image you are trying to portray.

Look at the resources you need to support any social media campaigns. With the use of reports, it can take time to analyse statistics and results. This means identifying the number and type of people who can help support this area. Establish who is best qualified internally to do this type of follow-up work to ensure that you have the mechanics in place for any campaign. This might involve some additional training for anyone who might not be a specialist in social media, or in how you want to run a particular campaign.

Differentiate between broadcasting your brand messages and communicating information and news to your target audience. For example, are you promoting your company, particular products and services or an interactive discussion about a relevant topic or your expertise in it? This will make it easier to align the type of communication you want with the expected outcome.

The impact of social media on consumers

Having a social media strategy involves thinking carefully about what type of interaction you want with users of the network you choose to engage with. If you decide to advertise, you will need to use tools to measure your campaign success. This is covered in more detail in *Chapter 6, Getting the best out of data analytics*. If you are looking for conversations and a two-way engagement, then think carefully about your tactics and content.

A comment on social media can be communicated quickly and to many users. This has the potential to greatly affect a large number of people's perception of that brand and other brands a company sells. In 2016, with over 2.3 billion global social media users alone, this is a very powerful collective audience and one which is growing.

Users have the ability to share information and get other people to post their opinions in real time. This has helped to create a new type of environment, where companies have needed to be more mindful about how they communicate information. They also need to be prepared to react to any criticism which could be damaging.

Individual opinions now have the ability to enhance or damage a company's brand and its reputation. Social media networks have transformed the way our society views what we buy and how we are sold to. People can post a message or a review and put a company under pressure to act, especially if others endorse the same view.

However, the effect of social media on society and on consumers has enabled companies to be more aware of what customers actually want. This makes planning to help provide the right products easier to identify and fulfil. Most importantly, it has allowed companies to redefine the components of a successful customer-supplier relationship. Marketers can break down the process of purchasing to suit a digital age.

In order to manage the two-way interaction between supplier and customer, marketing departments need to prepare new engagements on a regular basis. It means that marketers need a plan to deal with the potential challenges that emanate from this type of communication carefully; it will then be easier to build your brand and your company's image.

KEY QUESTIONS

- What elements have you put into a social media strategy?
- Which social media networks give you the best ROI and why?
- How often do you review your social media engagement?

Chapter summary

Social media has dramatically changed the way in which companies have approached marketing. Potential customers of products and services have become more aware of different brands through joining social media networks and getting involved in conversations. This has meant that many people in both B2B and B2C markets have become more communicative in the process. This applies both before and after a sale, with opinions that can be shared across a network.

For companies that decide to advertise and develop regular online communication, think carefully about your marketing message as well as your ROI.

Developing a social media strategy has enabled companies to plan with more confidence and engage with specific types of user. They can now get their messages across to a wider target audience in a flexible and potentially low-cost way. It allows campaigns to be tailored to a particular market or age-related audience. This can help companies who sell online where consumers share information and opinions about actual purchases with a large, often like-minded audience.

With the continued growth of social media, having a presence is an important part of any marketing strategy.

Key points

✓ Get to know the potential different social media platforms have for digital marketing

✓ Take the time to keep up to date with conversations and trends

✓ Think about which networks are likely to offer you the best return on ad spend

✓ Think about the type of interaction you want from social media

✓ Create a social media strategy that forms part of your digital marketing strategy

SIX
GETTING THE BEST OUT
OF DATA ANALYTICS

Introduction

Getting more 'hits' on your website and increasing traffic from digital marketing campaigns is something that every marketer aspires to achieving. This chapter looks at how you can improve your return on investment (ROI) by getting the best out of data analytics, that is the metrics which measure the success of your digital marketing.

We will cover web analytics and what Google, as the market leader, offers and how they approach analysing video, mobile and email campaigns. We will include the growing area of social media analytics and the type of measurement and tools available. We will also look at the criteria you can use as part of the measurement process.

The topics of SEO and PPC will help you to determine if you are getting the best out of any digital marketing spend. This includes defining a process in order to maximise the SEO process as well as looking at the value of Google AdWords. Finally, the chapter will cover the growth of social influence and how it has become something which marketers are using in order to try and promote their brands.

Marketing data analytics

Measurement

Marketing data analytics is the process of studying data in relation to website traffic, interactions, marketing initiatives and digital marketing campaigns. It covers areas like:

- Google and other web analytics

- Social analytics (Facebook, Twitter, Instagram etc.)

- Mobile and video analytics

- Email marketing

In order to get the best value for money, you will need to create a measurement process. This will allow you to analyse the results of your campaigns and help you to see which areas have provided the best value and give the best ROI. It should include looking at industry trends and past campaigns so that comparisons and learning points can be made. This will help you to make the best use of what you need for the future rather than relying on historical information alone to make decisions.

Measurement criteria can be broken down into areas like social media growth, PPC, SEO, lead conversion and Click Through Rates (CTRs) – the percentage of people who received your message and clicked on a link. This will add value in helping you to look at how successful your campaigns are and whether they are the right ones.

Another area to look at is audience segmentation which allows you to divide clusters of your target customers into categories. It will help you drive marketing messages to different segments which will improve key areas like conversion rates and the quality of responses.

In recent years, digital marketing has expanded to a point where many new channels have opened up. The performance of these channels needs to be analysed to see how effective they are in order to establish which ones are the best to invest time and money in.

If you sell online, you will want to establish a ratio between what has been invested in digital marketing and what volume of sales were achieved. This involves monitoring the behaviour of your customers in relation to how much they buy and how much time potential customers spend on your website. This is known as the customer acquisition cost and should always be lower than the lifetime value of the customer, i.e. the amount you gain from a customer over time.

You can then use web analytic tools to drill down to specific areas to see what is working and what isn't. This will help you to repeat any success in the future as well as change any content which isn't being viewed. The biggest web analytics service you can use, free of charge, is Google Analytics.

Google Analytics and other web analytics

Google Analytics offers statistics regarding the number of visitors to a website or mobile app. It gives very useful information on:

- Site visits – audience engagement

- Average visit duration (and for mobile)

- Goal conversion rates

- Page views (and for mobile) – you want a user to view several pages

- Bounce rates – you want to aim for a low 'bounce' rate, i.e. the percentage of visitors who visited your site but left after viewing only one page

- Percentage of new visits

- Visit duration per country/territory

- Visits and page views by traffic type

- Most engaged content

Google can track referral traffic from any URL (Uniform Resource Locator – a unique web address to access a file). It provides a dashboard to view its data analytics results, an example of which can be illustrated in following way:

GOOGLE ANALYTICS DASHBOARD

Google also offers a subscription-based service (Google Analytics 360 Suite) which has a higher level of sophistication. It is designed for larger companies and those with higher amounts of website traffic, i.e. number of visits, clicks, time spent on a page.

Microsoft's search engine, Bing, also has data analytics that can help you improve your search results. It is more about getting the best from your advertising campaigns and it offers to track events and integrate them within any Bing Ads. It can produce digital marketing campaign reports using Bing Ads to measure results and Microsoft's Bing Webmaster Tools can give you traffic insights and help improve the stability of your website through its tools, much like Google's Search Console.

There are other methods which offer alternatives, many of which are subscription-based but some of which are free. These include:

- **Rankwatch** (subscription) – shows Google ranking metrics to measure SEO

- **Mixpanel** (free with a more enhanced version on subscription) – good with mobile and real-time information

- **Kissmetrics** (subscription) – focuses on people's data, i.e. what they do on your website

- **Clicky** (subscription) – good visuals with heat maps and a Twitter monitoring feature

- **Woopra** (subscription) – similar to Kissmetric, focuses on your customer engagement

- **SEMrush** – offers a suite for online marketing, from SEO and PPC to social media and video advertising research

Companies offering subscription and free data analytics can change over time. You might find others not listed here more or less suited to your own needs, i.e. ones which specialise in video analytics.

Mobile and video analytics

In relation to mobile and video analytics, there are a number of companies that offer tools. YouTube offers video channel performance measurement in the way of reports and metrics which cover areas like how many people watched a video and for how long. It enables you to compare visits to future sales conversions by tracking the number of leads you get. Mixpanel is another which is seen as a leading mobile app analytics tool (mixpanel.com).

Email marketing

There are several email marketing platforms, from MailChimp – a point-and-click email builder, to Mailgun – the email service created for web developers. With email marketing, think about how realistic your goals are and the conversion rates you expect. Click through rates (CTRs) give a good indication as to how many people are actually reading the content of the email as well as which content is getting the best attention. Other obvious metrics which you should use in any email marketing campaign include conversion and bounce rates.

Conversion rates are the percentage of people who received your email and clicked on a link. Bounce rates are the percentage of email addresses that didn't receive your message. They can be used to establish how successful the delivery of emails actually was. If you aren't happy with this percentage, go back to how your database of email addresses was formulated and remove them. You also don't want to find that your emails are constantly being received as spam! Look to improve this for the future through better validation and the use of keywords in campaigns.

Other areas that you should look at include recipients who forwarded an email on to someone or posted it on social media. By encouraging people to do this, you will increase your reach, your brand authority and your social media presence – providing that the post was positive. By taking the time to establish your metrics for email campaigns, you stand a better chance of knowing what the ROI is.

Social media analytics

Social media networks were covered in *Chapter 5, Platforms for digital marketing communication*. These can gather data from websites for marketers to use to help determine the volume of traffic and in which areas. This can make it easier to make business decisions about the future type of digital marketing campaigns you need. There are many providers of social media analytics, for example:

- **Agorapulse** – enables you to manage social media sites like Facebook and Twitter in one place

- **Constant Contact** – helps digital consultants to support SME clients with some business marketing tools

- **Commun.it** – Facebook and Twitter management tool for community use

- **Hootsuite Ads** – automated with Facebook to search for best posts to advertise

- **Upcast** – Works with Facebook and Twitter to offer third-party tracking and ad scheduling

- **Iconosquare** – Instagram management tool

Google Analytics also provides social media analytics within its platform. This will help you establish the number of visits from each major social network as well as shared content and the location of social media visitors.

The biggest social media platforms like Facebook, Twitter and LinkedIn have their own tools. Facebook Insights tracks user interaction with active users. It helps to determine which pages are being viewed the most and the time of day when users visit the site. It also looks at the type of content being viewed which can help you determine what type to display. You can see the number of engagements a user has along with their age group. This can be useful in analysing your success in target markets.

Twitter Analytics provides a report on followers and tweets which includes knowing the number of interactions someone has made. YouTube Analytics helps you analyse and monitor channel performance and can be accessed on mobile devices. LinkedIn Analytics offers a number of ways in which users can analyse data relating to the traffic on its platform, for example:

- Identifying key trends

- Helping to measure the strength of individual posts

- Understanding more about your followers and their sources

- Metrics about activity and performance

- Helping connect to new people leading to more business opportunities

Social media analytics can help you to find out more about the interaction you have on a number of networks. This information will enable you to adapt your content, messages and focus so that you develop a strategy which engages your target audience. Many people feel that they can be more assertive and forthright on social media so, by monitoring information on it, you are likely to get feedback about how people feel about your products/services and brand(s).

In order to improve the engagement with your target audience through social media analytics, think about how you can achieve:

- Better satisfaction ratings

- Higher productivity

- Increased sales

This can be illustrated in the following way:

THE VALUE OF SOCIAL MEDIA ANALYTICS

Keep your core message the same across different social media platforms whether you're sharing content through email newsletters, Twitter or Facebook. Do adapt it, however, to the platform you are using; for example, on Instagram you will use an image, Facebook will be more conversational and Twitter will be more of a broadcast.

By having an agreed process to manage your social media engagement, you can get the best out of it. This will improve your digital marketing activities and sales performance. It will also allow you to identify any channel deficiencies in order to make the necessary changes for future social media initiatives.

Other tools

Digital marketing tools and apps can provide expertise to help support you in areas like SEO, content marketing, visualisation and publishing. It is a good idea to categorise what a particular tool can help you with, for example:

- Understand customer search (engine) behaviour

- Look for the latest developments in your particular market

- Focus on benchmarking your competitors

- Manage social media updates

- Find people or companies that you want to influence

- Analyse backlinks for SEO

These tools are specifically designed to get a general overview of how effective your online marketing is and they will help the measurement process. Be mindful of which ones you choose and how many you really need. Some of them are free but it is worth establishing first what you actually want to achieve in order to ensure that you use the right ones. Here are some examples of the tools available to you:

SEO tools

- **Varvy** – gives an overview of any website

- **Soovle** – allows you to use different search engines to look for related search terms

- **Moz Pro** – allows you to track and rank pages and keywords

Content marketing tools

- **HubSpot** – helps companies attract visitors, convert leads and close customers

- **Curata** – a content marketing platform to track leads and analyse content

- **Storify** – uses a single search engine to search and share content on social networks

- **Venngage** – makes infographics creation easier

- **Pocket** – enables you to save articles, pictures and video content for later use

Ad management

- **Marin Software** – a bid management PPC tool

- **Epom** – helps supervise configuration and optimisation of ad campaigns

Whatever tools you decide to use that work, consistency is essential. This will help you track results over time which will give you a better indication of any trends that exist.

Marketing analytics can help you to understand your performance in relation to your website and your interaction with social networks. This can help improve your decision-making when it comes to your future marketing spend and increase your sales conversions.

SEO and PPC

SEO

Search Engine Optimisation (SEO) is a digital marketing mechanism for growing visibility in a more organic and non-chargeable way (compared to PPC). It looks at the types of words on a website page relevant to what the site is offering. It includes technical and creative elements in order to drive traffic to your website and helps to increase awareness in search engines.

Search engines (like Google, Bing and Yahoo) look for the quality of content and how your website is structured to establish its level of authority. In order to help you increase your rankings, use words based on their potential impact. If you don't focus on SEO, then a search on your products or services can get lost when compared to your competitors.

SEO within marketing has changed over the past few years. It is more focused now on driving traffic and maximising the number of conversions. Keywords and phrases are important in order to attract hits to a website as well as the number of backlinks, ideally from highly ranked websites, which help improve your website's authority.

Search engine traffic is used far more now with mobile searches due to the increase in mobile phones and tablets. This means that companies need to think about how to target mobile users, i.e. shorter content than for a desktop or laptop user.

Google advises that to get the best out of your mobile searches you should build a responsive web design (google.com). This should include letting search engines know when a page is formatted for mobile use and make sure the content, like video, plays well on a mobile or tablet (regardless of whether you have iOS or Android as the operating system). You can use tools like Google Webmaster, Bing Webmaster or Yahoo Webmaster.

You need to think about images too as they have become more prevalent on websites along with the use of video. They can be used to target mobile users as part of a marketing campaign. For example, it is often easier to watch a 30-second advert on video than read a one-page document or web page.

SEO can be improved with the use of social media. Anything which is popular on social media is often used by search engines as part of their ranking. Also, it's important to focus on the user experience once someone goes to your website, rather than just the content itself. A website with a good user experience will improve a user's 'dwell time' (the time spent on a particular page), which is considered favourably by search engines.

Tell a 'story' to engage with people on your website and also disseminate this through social media. You should look at paying for keywords with PPC and then use paid advertising to better manage your SEO strategy. SEO will take time to establish, often more than six months to see some real progress. But the value can be more 'hits' on your website or more communication from interested prospects.

'Internal linking' can improve the customer experience as well as allowing search engines to 'crawl' your website. This involves browsing the website and indexing the content, including its assets such as video and images. This helps when people specify image or video searches in search engines. Other areas to focus on include the content headers you put on your website and highlighted content. Search engines will pick up on this relevant content in much the same way as when you scan a newspaper and notice the headlines. They will use these as primary keywords so the better your headlines, the more chance they have of being picked up by people doing a web search. But you need to be careful not to over-promise when trying to entice people to your website or you may find that although you get more traffic, this is not converted into interest or future sales.

This means that the content on your website needs to be carefully thought through as well as the photos/images you use. Also, 'keyword stuffing' (when a web page is loaded with keywords designed to manipulate a site's ranking in Google) can penalise your searches if Google considers that you are using this for gaming purposes.

The process of creating an SEO campaign, implementing it, managing it and reviewing it is something that you should formalise. This can be seen in the following way:

You may decide to choose different parameters and in a slightly different order, but take the time to create a path that can become part of your SEO process. Each part of this requires involving relevant people to progress the relevant actions.

1 **Research/set goals** – this will help you to compare plans with outcomes

2 **Competitor analysis** – essential to ensure you focus on your USPs

3 **Website design** – think about this from a keywords and navigation perspective

4 **Web tools** – decide which ones you want to use and the metrics

5 **Keyword search** – important to select and prioritise

6 **Website content** – think about value to the customer

7 **Social media** – choose platforms and strategy

8 **Optimisation** – look at how this can be achieved

9 **Build backlinks** – choose web links from relevant sources to your relevant web page

10 **Analysis and review** – this will help you to refine and progress

To get the best out of SEO, create original quality content on your website and do this frequently dependant on your resources. Consider creating 'evergreen content', i.e. content that is continually relevant and stays 'fresh' for your users. You should look at engaging with the top five social media networks and keep up to date with your market to give examples of best practice. This will help keep your content new and improve its potential appeal.

PPC

Pay Per Click (PPC) is a model in which advertisers pay a fee every time someone clicks on an advert, e.g. in Google AdWords. This means that you are paying for someone to click on an advert link rather than growing interest organically like through SEO. One of the most popular forms of PPC is search engine advertising. This allows you to pick keywords which people type into search engines in order to try and attract people to your website. Every time someone clicks on your link, you would need to pay a fee to the search engine.

It's advisable to create specific landing pages for your ads. By doing this, search engines will reward you for marketing campaigns as they measure this type of structured approach by charging less per click. They do this by calculating how landing pages (and other specific pages which relate to a search) are structured and which keywords are relevant. This also maximises the user experience.

You should create a PPC process similar to the one used for SEO and this will involve the paid element per click in, for example, Google AdWords (which is covered in the next section). A PPC campaign involves using the best/most relevant keywords you can, but be sure to uses a keyword analysis tool to make sure you can optimise your content at a reasonable fee. They need to be put into a well-structured digital marketing campaign. You can then put this into an 'ad group', i.e. a group of one or more ads that share a set of keywords.

You set a price which can be used when your ad group's keywords activate an ad to appear. This is known as a Cost Per Click (CPC). You then need to measure your conversion rates. In order to maximise your investment in PPC, you need to research and select the right keywords. These need to be organised into a marketing campaign and in Google measure how well you meet certain criteria, for example if your ads and landing pages satisfy users.

Google AdWords

Google AdWords is a pay-and-display advertising service. It is the most popular PPC advertising method, which is why many companies use Google as their search engine of choice to advertise with. It works on a PPC model where users bid on keywords and then pay for every click on their ads.

Each time a search is initiated with Google it looks at its advertisers and selects a set of 'winners' who will appear on the search result page. They are chosen for a number of items, for example keywords, ad campaigns and the size of keyword bids. An Ad Rank list is a way of knowing who has the highest ranking status. This is done through a metric which calculates two important factors: a CPC bid – which is the highest amount someone is prepared to bid, including a click-through rate relevance – and a landing page quality score.

The benefit from a digital marketing perspective is that this allows advertisers to define their budget and target potential customers/accounts within these boundaries. In order to get the best out of any PPC marketing campaign you should:

- Think carefully about the keywords you choose

- Choose smaller ad groups that are relevant to your target audience

- Adapt your own landing pages to align with potential search engine words

- Make a decision about how much you are prepared to spend on a keyword

As with any digital marketing campaign, you should review your metrics. This will ensure that the money you spend and the effort you make is producing results. Take the time to analyse your performance so that you can determine what areas you might need to change. This will help you get the best out of your budget and maximise your conversion rates.

KEY QUESTIONS

- What criteria do you use to decide how much to invest in SEO and PPC?

- How often do you review your spend with this?

Social influencer marketing

Social influence marketing (or influencer marketing) is relatively new and is designed to target key individuals rather than those in a particular market sector. The focus is on using the influence that someone has (or a group has) on a particular topic to encourage potential customers to buy your products or services.

Social influence derives from someone's market reach which has been gained via their knowledge, experience and profile. Depending on the brand, influence can be from within a particular market or someone with a celebrity status. The main issue is this person's ability to give a brand an endorsement which is credible and has authority. This in turn helps to persuade people that the brand is worth investigating and, ultimately, purchasing. It is different from being a brand ambassador which is, in effect, a contracted freelance role.

In order to help people better understand the credibility and measurement of social influence, companies like Klout have developed an interesting business model. Klout is a web and mobile app that looks to measure a level of influence by giving a score out of 100. It does this by searching social media channels (klout.com). Tools like BuzzSumo, Kred, PeerIndex and SproutSocial can also help identify someone's level of social influence.

Many potential buyers often prefer personal recommendation or referral (known as word-of-mouth marketing – WOMM) when making future purchasing decisions. Neilsen's research stated that more than eight out of ten respondents either 'somewhat or completely trusted the recommendations of friends and family' (nielsen.com).

This shows that you need to think about who you want to help to promote your brand and what type of influence you think that person has. If you want to lead social influence in relation to marketing, think about the strength of your USPs. This will help you merge the challenging concepts of individuality, popularity and credibility. In order to try and achieve this, think about the following areas:

- Demonstrate that you have interesting, engaging and relevant content on your website and social media platforms

- Don't follow trends which can become outdated; look at what your brand stands for and take the time to engage with the types of digital marketing which really promote it

- Get feedback from your customers so that you can review your level of social influence

- Look at what your competitors are doing; this will help you to make decisions about how you position your brand and the type of social influence you need

- Try and be the first to disseminate stories across the social side of the Web

It is the sharing of information and the online social media networks that have enabled influencer marketing to grow. Credibility can be gained by having a high volume of traffic as well as quality of followers (on Facebook, for example). This can give status to your users and your brand. It can also help with social influence to promote a positive engagement with your target audience.

KEY QUESTIONS

- How much do you know about social influencer marketing?
- What focus have you given to it?

Chapter summary

Marketing data analytics can take time to understand and you need to break down the component parts in order to know how to get the best ROI. But taking the time to get this right can provide you with the right information to make decisions about your digital marketing campaigns. Analytical tools from Google and other providers can help you to optimise campaigns while allowing you to make decisions about what works and what doesn't.

You need to think about social media networks and the analytics they offer so that you get the best out of each one. This will help you to make changes relatively quickly and focus on the areas that are the most productive. Also, think carefully about SEO and PPC in order to get the best exposure you can on search engine results pages. Using the right words and phrases and having a strategy to manage this is essential if you are going to maximise your spend.

Finally, think about how the Web is changing and how you can use social influence to really engage with your target audience. Digital marketing now has more emphasis on how to better manage potential customer engagement and interaction. Be part of this by getting involved in discussions on social media as well as direct email contact and regularly updated blogs. This will show your target audience that you are a key player in the topics that you want to promote, which in turn will help to promote your brand(s).

Key points

✓ Use Google and other web analytics to provide a process you can measure

✓ Engage with social media analytics to help you focus on the right channels

✓ Think about what other tools can support your analytics

✓ Review any investment you make in SEO and PPC in order to get the best return

✓ Look at how you can use social influence to engage with your target audience

SEVEN

INTEGRATING WITH TRADITIONAL FORMS OF MARKETING

CHAPTER TOPICS

- The Marketing Mix
- Traditional forms of marketing
- Traditional versus new media channels

Introduction

Digital marketing has revolutionised the way many companies communicate information about their products and services. Its ability to use a more targeted approach and the rise of social media has made it easier to engage with people. It has in many instances given a better return on investment (ROI), compared with traditional forms of marketing.

This chapter will look at what factors to consider when you are promoting a brand. It will focus on getting you to think about which types of marketing work best.

Many companies still spend vast amounts of money on traditional forms of marketing. We will explore the main types of traditional marketing, how they still have an important role to play and why companies need to use them. We will also look at how a combined approach in some markets can be better than focusing on traditional or digital elements alone as part of a campaign strategy.

The Marketing Mix

In order to get a realistic perspective, it is a good idea to look at the four main areas that underpin traditional forms of marketing. The Marketing Mix is a well-known concept originated by Neil H Borden, former president of the American Marketing Association (AMA). It has four parts to it that make up a brand's offer. They are:

- Product

- Price

- Place

- Promotion

The product represents what you are looking to sell; the price is what the product is to be sold for; the place is how you intend to get the product to market and the distribution channel(s) you intend to use to access it; promotion looks at how you intend to get the attention of your target audience.

There are other factors that relate to these four elements and the model has been updated to include them: for example process, people and physical environment. However, these four remain a powerful way of focusing on some of the main areas which you need to get right in order to successfully market a product or service.

This can be illustrated in the following way by:

THE MARKETING MIX

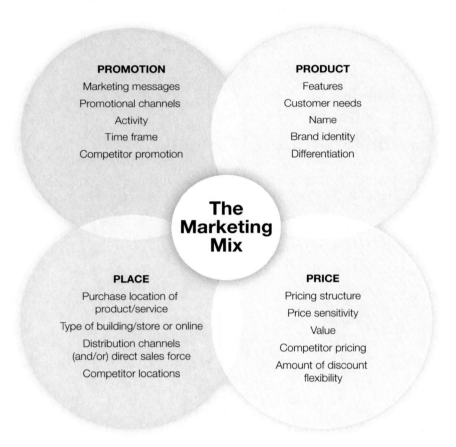

PROMOTION
Marketing messages
Promotional channels
Activity
Time frame
Competitor promotion

PRODUCT
Features
Customer needs
Name
Brand identity
Differentiation

The Marketing Mix

PLACE
Purchase location of
product/service
Type of building/store or online
Distribution channels
(and/or) direct sales force
Competitor locations

PRICE
Pricing structure
Price sensitivity
Value
Competitor pricing
Amount of discount
flexibility

The Marketing Mix is a good way to plan your route to market and ensure that you have the right focus in the areas it covers. It allows for experimentation and will involve some market research. However, the right mix is what each marketing strategy depends upon. As part of this, you need to think about the message you are trying to convey as part of a campaign so that it resonates with people to improve your brand awareness.

Traditional forms of marketing

There are a number of ways to use traditional forms of marketing in relation to B2B or B2C. This can be illustrated in the following way:

TRADITIONAL MARKETING

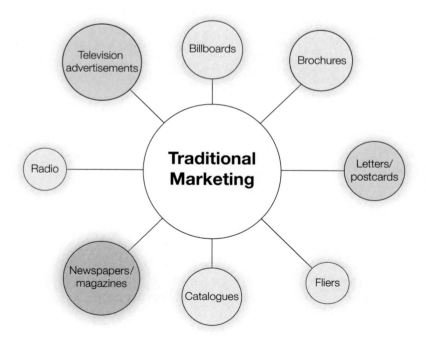

These traditional forms of marketing have been used for many years and buyers are familiar with them. You should take the time to look at each type to determine whether it is worth investing in.

Advertising

Both television and radio advertising are popular and successful forms of marketing. They have the potential to reach a wide audience, although for a limited period of time. On television, advertising can be tailored to an audience and they can see how a product works and the value of the brand can be easily articulated.

With radio advertising, campaigns can be targeted in a specific geographical area and to a particular market. However, television adverts can be communicated internationally, nationally or locally. Although for international advertisements language, cultural differences and humour need to be factored in.

Television advertising is more costly than other traditional forms of marketing, although there is considerable value in having the potential of a large and targeted audience. By using visual and audio to communicate the message, it allows a higher degree of sophistication in terms of creativity.

You can of course advertise in newspapers and magazines, many of which can be related to a particular market – for example, a magazine designed for the insurance industry. As with digital marketing, you need to differentiate yourself in order to articulate your value proposition.

Direct marketing

Another type of traditional marketing comes in the form of direct mail, which is posted or delivered to a company or individual. It can include:

- Brochures

- Letters

- Postcards

- Flyers

- Catalogues

This type of marketing can be effective if it hits the right target audience but, to recipients who do not see the value, it can be received in the same way that spam is when receiving emails. However, its strengths are in its directness and focus.

Marketing directly to a company or individual is still a popular form of advertising. If a campaign is successful, it can often be because it was personalised. This can help to create stronger brand recognition, even if it takes more time to plan, and has the following benefits:

- You can direct your message to a particular market and your target audience

- You can get feedback to help review the strength of a campaign, product or service

- It allows companies to test a market by gauging interest in future products

Direct marketing is an important part of traditional marketing and has grown significantly in the past 25 years. The increased use of technology has allowed marketers to be more precise in the targeting and measurement of campaigns.

Cold calling

Another form of traditional marketing is the cold call. It is much maligned because it can be intrusive and unwanted. However, some call centres exist to make contact with potential new customers or to call existing ones to introduce new products and services.

The cost of telephoning has significantly reduced, allowing more affordable campaigns. It has also enabled more sophistication in the building of databases as well as creating call centres to better manage the follow-up process.

Cold calling is a skill and a 'numbers game' and while it can be effective, the returns need to be carefully measured. This is because for every successful call there are likely to be a high number which have the potential to alienate the person receiving it which, in turn, can have a negative effect on the brand which is being promoted.

Cold calling often works better when it is part of a direct marketing campaign through a follow-up call. By doing this, there is a better chance of articulating the value of a product or service if the recipient agrees to engage in a conversation. You can also answer any potential objections or concerns giving you more control over the sales process. Many people receiving unsolicited calls don't like this type of communication, however, and find it intrusive.

Conference, exhibition or trade show

A conference, exhibition or trade show has the ability for potential customers to proactively visit an industry or product-specific event. This is good news for the vendors as they are likely to be well received by the visitors to their stands. There is no commitment offered from potential customers but there is normally a relatively high degree of the following:

- Interaction between buyer and seller

- Information gathering

- Questions that can be answered directly by the seller

- Brand promotion

- Discussion about latest techniques, trends, products and solutions

It can take sellers time to encourage potential buyers to come to these types of events. Sometimes an event doesn't need this type of promotion because it can be a useful way of keeping in touch with a particular industry. Also, if a well-known multinational company is taking part in an exhibition, people might come due to its name, reputation or interest in new products and services.

If these types of events are planned well they can be successful as a way of increasing brand awareness and communicating with your target audience.

Referrals and introductions

For most companies, there is nothing better than getting a referral as a lead. This is because someone else is endorsing your product or service and introducing that company or person directly to you. A 'warm' introduction is one built on trust with the introducer. 'Word of mouth' is another way in which new people might hear about you and want to get in touch.

Good direct referrals make it easier to both gain customers and keep them. If someone you know has used a product and likes it, this makes your own buying decision more straightforward. You can ask the referrer all the questions you want to know in advance and get an answer from a user's perspective. Referrals are not easy to obtain, unless you ask existing customers/clients for them, but they are great forms of lead generation if you can invest the time to obtain them.

Networking

Networking events have become very popular. They normally involve a group of professionals getting together to listen to a speaker and socialise before and afterwards. The reason for going might be the types of people that you can meet as well as some common interest in a particular market, subject or group of people.

Networking is often approached in the best way by looking at how you can genuinely help someone. That approach builds up trust and confidence and, if you meet someone regularly at a local event, it is easier to develop some type of business relationship with that person.

Who uses traditional marketing?

Traditional forms of marketing are used by most companies today, especially advertising. Due to the cost, television advertising is more likely to be used by large and multinational companies. However, SMEs might use local newspapers, magazines and radio as part of their traditional marketing budget spend.

Traditional versus new marketing channels

Although the strategies of companies in relation to marketing have changed since the Web was introduced, many of the basic concepts of marketing haven't. Companies still need to:

- Identify a target market

- Have a campaign focus

- Create a message for the target audience

- Communicate the brand message through a channel

Technology has created a massive shift in consumer expectation in the last decade. People have much more information available to them and are far more aware of how to access it. In the B2C market, consumers can also buy a huge amount of products online. This has meant that companies have had to adapt to this by:

- Looking at the value of traditional and digital forms of marketing

- Making a choice as to which brands to spend a budget on

With all types of marketing, you need to look at the process from an initial campaign to a purchase and any post-sales business relationship. The marketing funnel is an additional way to view the path taken to track an engagement with potential buyers. It can be used in a slightly different way to the customer buying cycle illustrated in *Chapter 3, Changes that impact on the customer experience*.

The marketing funnel is useful to plan activity and monitor what needs to be done at each stage in relation to a buyer's decision making. It can be viewed from both marketing and buying points of view. This can help to better structure marketing campaigns and look at what actions and outcomes to measure at different stages. It can be illustrated in the following way:

THE MARKETING FUNNEL

Marketing campaigns

Awareness
(of brand)

Interest
(in product/service)

Evaluation
(of product/service)

Commitment
(to purchase)

Loyalty
(+ referrals)

Advocacy

Marketers need to break down the needs of a potential customer and look for emotional ties they might have with a particular brand. This includes what 'triggers' them to move from stage to stage before, during and after a purchase has taken place. This is made more interesting in light of competitor activity and a customer's decision-making process.

However, traditional marketing has not died even though it is in decline. But it does need to compete with other potentially more cost-effective types of campaign. To support this, it is predicted that traditional forms of marketing like television and newspapers will form approximately 55 per cent of US advertising spend by 2020 (emarketer.com).

Television advertising globally is likely to increase to nearly $210 billion by 2020 (statista.com). If this is the case, it confirms that this traditional form of advertising alone is likely to continue to be a bigger player than the entire digital marketing spend for the same year. The format of advertising has changed and a transition to digital marketing from some areas of traditional marketing is on the increase. But we mustn't forget the power of other forms of traditional marketing, particularly television advertising and its own potential growth.

Applying traditional marketing skills

As with digital forms of marketing, you should ensure that you communicate the USP that your brand has. For example:

- Are you offering a more cost-effective solution?

- Are your products of a better quality than your competitors?

- Are you offering something which other companies in your market don't?

- Is your service better in some way than other companies? If so how?

It is unlikely that you will have a unique selling point (USP), rather something that distinguishes you from your competitors, but it is important to articulate this to your prospective customers so that they are aware of the value of your proposition.

There can be campaigns where companies don't always reinforce some type of USP and this could be a lost opportunity. If you compare two companies who both have a similar USP but one doesn't promote it well and the other does, it is more likely that the latter will be the one who gets remembered. That is why you need to ensure that you plan this as part of your marketing communication.

One of the challenges that companies now face is what proportion of their marketing budget to spend on traditional and digital marketing platforms. Television advertising is expensive but this still leaves decisions to be made about the other types of marketing. In most surveys, traditional forms still feature in a top ten of total marketing spend. This applies even if the amount and percentage of spend has decreased in favour of digital marketing.

What to focus on

A combined marketing approach can often help companies find more qualified prospects leading to higher sales from marketing campaigns. This depends on the size of your company and whether you have a dedicated marketing department and budget. Whatever your situation is, you need to determine the level of sales and ROI you expect to gain.

Another factor to consider is the time it will take to plan a campaign. You may have an annual budget which includes a number of regular campaigns focused on particular months or events. Many campaigns focus on the seasonal aspect of products, while others might concentrate more on their selling history to establish when the best time is to market particular areas.

In terms of planning a traditional marketing campaign, think about the timescale, who needs to be involved and if the resources you have are going to be sufficient to make it a success. For example, advertising in a local magazine might need a few weeks' notice, if only because the advertising space could already have been booked up in advance. You should think about the type of materials and time needed for your marketing team to support this.

Public relations

While marketing looks at how to promote products and services, public relations (PR) focuses on how information can be used to enhance a company's reputation. Conferences and industry awards are examples of how credibility and values can be communicated. With the advance of digital technology, this is often channelled in the form of news on a company's website, email campaigns and through social media. All these types of PR help to support the marketing messages being created and are a vital part of increasing exposure.

Working together with traditional and digital marketing

The choice with traditional and digital marketing isn't always exclusively between old and new marketing concepts. You need to look at how well the two methods can work together and in what context they don't. This will require research to establish what channels you think best serve your own company.

The benefit of a combined approach is that you can look at what type of return you want from each method and plan your marketing around this. It doesn't have to be one way or the other. This gives you the benefits of mixing traditional methods like print advertising combined with something like a social media focus. Digital marketing can help to build awareness and develop business relationships and this can often underpin a more direct message with either a printed media or outbound telephone calling campaign.

While traditional forms of marketing are often seen as a way of reaching a broader but not so targeted audience, digital marketing enables you to be more specific. That is why many companies look for a combination of the two methods to maximise their marketing campaigns.

KEY QUESTIONS

- What stages does your own marketing funnel consist of?

- What percentage of traditional and digital marketing do you do?

- How do you manage the balance between traditional and digital marketing?

Chapter summary

Many smaller companies in particular, still rely heavily on traditional forms of marketing. However, SMEs and larger companies have moved towards a much higher investment in digital marketing. Whatever you decide to do, think about how to get the best out of your own marketing mix.

Don't discard traditional marketing if it can help you reach your target audience and gives you a good return, but be mindful that you still need to create and monitor some type of measurement process to establish your ROI with any budget spend. This is more challenging with some aspects of traditional marketing. Think about which marketing methods to use and test them out.

Finally, take the time to look at how you can get the best ROI from your marketing. This might involve a combined approach with traditional and digital marketing. If not, then have a measurement process in place so that you make planning decisions based on the best methods to engage with your target audience.

Key points

✓ Think about how well you cover the elements of The Marketing Mix

✓ Look at what traditional forms of marketing can work for you

✓ Assess the benefits of direct marketing and how to apply them well

✓ Think of whether traditional and digital marketing can work together for you

EIGHT
A MOVE TO INTERNATIONAL MARKETS

Introduction

It can be a daunting task to look at how a company can establish itself internationally. Decisions about what type of digital marketing to invest in and how much to spend are key factors which need researching. This chapter looks at some of the main areas that you will need to focus on if you want to sell in international markets.

We will look at many of the factors involved in creating a process and structure for doing so. This will cover how to compete with multinational companies and look at the types of value proposition you will need. The importance of creating a strategy which deals with the additional complexity of trading in different countries is covered. This includes the need to adapt to international markets and to being aware of the types of opportunities as well as threats that exist.

Finally, the chapter will deal with the need to monitor your progress as you trade in different countries so that you can be flexible if you have to change something. Applying digital marketing well in other countries provides real challenges that should be thought through carefully. By doing so, you will be in a better position to make this transition.

How to compete internationally

Before you decide to compete internationally look at the factors that are likely to affect you. Go through a process to establish what steps are needed to develop a strategy to support you. This will involve key people in sales, marketing, finance etc. To help with this, here is a brief checklist which covers some of the questions that will need answering.

No.	QUESTIONS CHECKLIST
1	What is the size of your domestic and new international target market?
2	Has your company reached a peak in the domestic market? (If yes, then is this the right time to think about competing internationally? If no, then what do you need to do to maintain growth in the domestic market)?
3	How do you plan to sell your products/services and support your brand(s)?
4	What research do you need to do and what partner relationships do you need to develop in order to prepare for this?
5	How far in advance has your company prepared for and is moving to international markets going to put pressure on your domestic market?

6	Does the company have the right resources to support an international sales and marketing presence, if so what are they?
7	What experience does the company have of international markets?
8	Which countries and regions internationally represent the best growth potential and what market conditions exist in each one?
9	What competitors exist internationally and what threat do they represent?
10	What budget and actions are needed in relation to digital marketing and to establishing a presence on social media platforms?

The answers to these questions and how they relate to your overall business goals will enable you to review your position before you make a decision to move to sell in other countries. The advent of digital marketing and its huge growth over the past few years has seen many small and medium-sized companies (SMEs) wanting to sell internationally. However, you will still need to look at a number of other areas in order to plan the resources you need, for example:

- Establishing whether your products or services are suitable for an international market

- Localisation (e.g. product labelling in the country's language)

- Setting up an export strategy

- Deciding if you need a commercial agent

- Deciding on the partner channels you intend to use

- Knowing who your end users are

- Understanding the costs and resources involved

You need to know the culture in the countries you are looking to sell into as well as the customs, laws and the way they trade. You can research this and look at the history of trading in your target markets. This should include information on your sales potential and the economic situation there, including what currency you intend trading in.

Think about which country or geographical area to target first. This will allow you time to adapt to any differences in the way you currently market your products and services. To become an international success, you have to understand how to penetrate new markets. This includes understanding what drives buying decisions in a particular country.

Look at the social and technological infrastructure and the impact it can have on how people use social media and engage with different brands. Find out who the key influencers are and what the local trends are in relation to buying decisions (Twitter can be a good resource for this). Take the time to find out what is popular on radio and television, what the online trends are and what devices are used.

Think about the needs of your potential customers and how they might differ internationally compared to a domestic market. How do you plan to actually sell your products and services, i.e. through partner channels or directly? These questions should form part of your strategy before you start any digital marketing campaigns.

Despite the set-up costs and the time and effort involved in planning, selling internationally has many advantages. For example, you can apply your digital marketing practices across different countries and maintain a consistent brand image. You should also be able to get economies of scale by having lower digital marketing costs. This collectively will help you to gain more credibility and experience as a supplier if you are successful.

You need to be aware of any differences in the business environment. These could include:

- The legal system

- Competitors

- Administrative procedures

- Brand communication

- Customer/consumer taste (depending on whether you are selling B2B or B2C).

You will also have to think about the marketing support structure you need in place and ways that you can attract new customers.

Competing with multinational companies

Multinational companies will already have the building blocks in place and the resources, experience, brand, history and product sales to support their credentials internationally. So, think about what you can do to establish yourself to be in a position to compete with them.

With the advent of digital technology, smaller companies are in a much better position to compete than ever before and there are a number of ways in which they can do this. SMEs often use digital marketing agencies rather than employ someone directly. This can help to give marketing support to promote products and services with expertise. It can also provide access to skills you need to give you scalability. This can be illustrated in the following way:

INTERNATIONAL MARKETING STRUCTURE

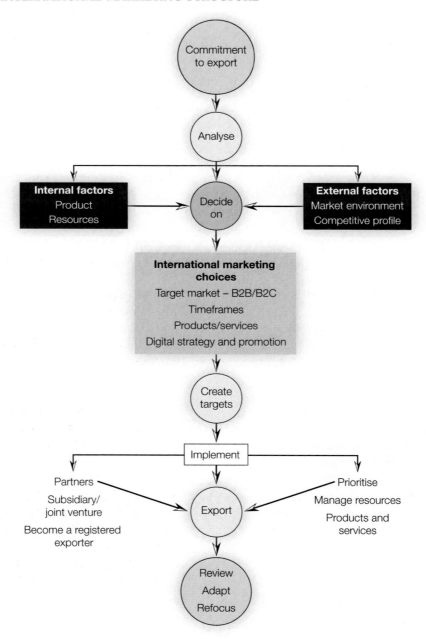

By having a structure to guide you, it will be easier to follow a logical path which covers the many important elements needed to trade successfully at an international level.

Enhancing your value proposition

When you are creating a structure, think about all the aspects you have been involved with in your dealings in your domestic market. Try and find what areas you think will and won't work. Talk to companies who have already done this and learn from their experience as well as the government department responsible for exports and international trade. This will give you as much information as possible in order to help you better understand the challenges involved.

Remember, what works in one market may not work in the same way in another. This means you will need to be flexible in your approach. You shouldn't expect to get everything right first time. Part of your plan could be to partner with local companies or use resellers. This will depend on the type of route to market you choose. For example, if you are selling products through resellers, a network will be essential. This will differ if you are selling a service over the Web or if you intend to sell directly to a consumer via your website.

You will need to look at the social media elements of your international target market. For example, how do networks like Facebook, YouTube, and LinkedIn perform in these countries? Social media is covered in more detail in *Chapter 5, Platforms for digital marketing communication.*

You will need to think about the task of translating your marketing information into the local language which will require expertise and support. Native speakers are important to engage with to get your message across in a credible way when you are translating text from one language to another. This will help to avoid any potential misunderstandings, which on social media in particular could be costly.

Ensure that you create a personal message, even if you don't have experience of the nuances of the language or culture. Don't assume that your digital message in one part of the world will necessarily translate well to a different geographical region.

Think about your brand and the messaging so it can apply to the country you are targeting. Be careful of using automated systems which recommend products as they can sometimes make mistakes! Your first experience needs to be a good one so take the time to do this well.

Again, for your value proposition to be understood and correctly articulated, you need to differentiate your company. Local companies may well already sell something similar to you, which is why having some good, easily understood unique selling points (USPs) is essential. Larger companies with an international presence won't need to sell themselves in the same way as a new company entering a market for the first time. With this in mind, you are unlikely to be able to compete on price as easily so articulating your value should be a top priority.

Finally, in a B2C market don't assume that most of your potential customers will be using a desktop computer, laptop or even a tablet. Many could well be using mobile phones to access the Web and social media websites. Check that mobile phone capability is optimised, Wi-Fi coverage is established and in which countries consumers use them in preference to other devices. This will save you time and help you be better prepared to compete.

KEY QUESTIONS

- How well equipped are you to trade internationally?
- How strong is your brand compared to multinational companies?
- What is your value proposition?

Having an international strategy

Many SMEs don't always take the time to think about an international strategy when they look to sell into other countries. This means that their potential to succeed can be limited. You don't have to be a multinational company to assess the size and potential of a particular market in a country or geographical region. But you do need to think about your target audience and how to adapt to it.

Before you sell internationally, you should first create a digital marketing strategy (this is covered in *Chapter 2, Creating a digital marketing strategy*). However, international marketing needs to incorporate additional factors in comparison to a domestic focus. You might want to visualise part of your plan by drawing a mind map, i.e. where ideas, goals and actions emanate from one central strategy. For example:

Creating an international strategy should involve topics like customer service and branding. You also need to think about the different regulations which a country might have that could affect you as well as finding out who is going to host your website. By taking the time to do this, you will not only save time in the long run but you will also save money.

You can improve your chances of success by defining the steps you want to take. It is better to assess risk and deal with it before you start trading in another country in order to maximise your chances of doing so with confidence.

In order to compete on the international stage, think about the following areas and then formalise them as part of your own international digital marketing strategy.

1. Ensure that your website has an international look and feel

Think about having more than one version of your website. You need to adapt this to different countries and individual cultural differences. This can involve symbols, colours, use of text and converting prices into local currencies. This might seem a lot of work but essentially the main area you'll need to change is the language.

You will need a good translator rather than a mechanised translation to achieve this and it helps to personalise the website. You also need to think about how long it takes to load a page in a particular country; this will probably require some help in order to maximise your optimisation.

2. Do research regarding potential traffic and profitability

You will need to know the potential numbers of people looking at your website and the amount of business in relation to future sales you can achieve. This will involve research in certain countries or even continents which you can incorporate into your strategy.

You will need to be able to analyse your web traffic and statistics from digital marketing campaigns per product and per country. This involves setting up the right metrics, which is covered in more detail in *Chapter 6, Getting the best out of data analytics*. There might also be seasonal trends to consider.

3. Take the time to tailor your web presence to your audience

This involves a split between targeting by country and by language. Once you have decided on the split, you need to be consistent so that your brand is easy to identify and follow.

4. Know what keywords to use

Taking the time to research popular keywords, especially in another language, can help improve any Search Engine Optimisation (SEO) you plan to do. This also applies to the social networks you use. It will help you better relate to your international target audience.

5. Encourage interaction

As in your domestic market, encourage users to interact with your company and brand(s) via your website. Make use of surveys, polls, requests to subscribe to your newsletter, blogs and even a questionnaire about the site's quality. It will encourage a two-way communication which could lead to more potential enquiries. Having enthusiasm and energy with regular, relevant and interesting mate-rial should make a good impression with your target audience.

Other factors that can affect your ability to trade successfully in an international market include:

- Having the right types of products and services

- Being innovative

- Building market share quickly

- Creating brand awareness

- Being competitive

These types of challenge will have an effect on a company's ability to build a successful brand and attract potential customers.

Adapting to a digital world

In many ways the digitisation of marketing has changed the nature of competition. Companies selling online have been able to undercut many traditional resellers and this has forced the latter to rethink how they market their products. There is so much information now for people to look at and digest, and mobile devices make the communication of information easily accessible on a worldwide scale.

This has caused a transition for many companies who sell on an international stage. They have had to look again at their marketplace and assess how to get the best out of the age of digitisation, which has helped to lower the cost of many elements of marketing and provide a more tailored approach.

However, with change often comes risk. Digitisation of marketing has also allowed competitors into markets where they would previously have been unable to compete at an international level. Also, some traditional forms of marketing are not guaranteed to work as effectively and can take more time and resource to manage.

Opportunities and threats

There are a number of threats that emanate from digital marketing which you should be aware of. For example, it has allowed smaller companies to compete by having the benefit of a website and trading directly with potential customers/consumers. Traditional methods of using resellers in local countries can sometimes be bypassed, cutting out the 'middle man'. Smaller companies can choose which products in a market to target with great flexibility and this can threaten larger multinationals.

Competition has become more intense for many companies who have seen an increased number of niche providers enter a market with reduced prices. Also, there are times when software has replaced the need for actual labour, again helping new companies to be competitive. This has led to more automation of services and back-end office functions.

Monitoring your progress

If your company has a digital marketing strategy, you will want to plan how you can monitor your progress as part of it. This is important so that you can decide what type of budget to set and measure your return on investment (ROI).

You will need to decide what tools you need to use to define outcomes, for example, Google Analytics. This is covered in more detail in *Chapter 6, Getting the best out of data analytics*. One of your goals might be to increase the amount of traffic which comes to your website by a certain percentage within a given time period and, if so, this needs to be tracked.

You should look at what investment and outcomes you have experienced with your digital marketing so far, domestically or in other countries. Look at what went well and what didn't and, most importantly, why? Choose a realistic time frame to monitor and set goals for this, ones which are measurable and which you can analyse. As part of the monitoring process, look at the resources you have so that you can plan how to use them effectively. There is always some risk involved in this because marketing trends can change quickly.

You need to look at the team of people involved in a digital marketing campaign to ensure that they have the skills to adapt to your needs.

Decide whether you have enough experience and skill 'in-house' or whether you need to outsource some or all of the marketing services.

You should monitor your social media campaigns including what type of networks you are going to use. You need to assess who will manage this. There are also some important questions you need to answer, for example:

- What support tools will you use as part of the measurement process?

- Do you need to save and archive data?

- What time frame will you need reports for, i.e. weekly, monthly, quarterly?

- Who is your target audience?

- Do you need a monitoring tool to integrate with your Customer Relationship Management (CRM) system?

Monitoring your competitors

Do research on the competitors in your target market. Look at their approach in a particular country, their market share and what you can do to position yourself against them. This will help you maximise the value of your brand(s) in order to position yourself in the best possible way. There are some more targeted ways in which you can get an insight into what your competitors are doing, for example:

- *Keep in touch with new content that is put on their website and any redesign*
  You can use Google Analytics to set up alerts for particular keywords and keep up with trends in website design.

- *Monitor social activity*
  You can look at any competitor's posts on social networks as a way of getting an insight into what information they are posting or sharing.

- *Read their updated posts*
  You can read blogs, newsletters, case studies and white papers to compare ideas regarding your own content.

- *Track new competitor links*
  You can track new links with a link research tool (e.g. Moz Pro) and discover content that has worked well for a competitor.

- *Research a competitor's most shared content*
  There are tools to allow you to share content by topic and brand (e.g. Rival IQ). These enable you to track all types of competitor information.

- *Uncover and track a competitor's keywords*
  There is software which will allow you to uncover keywords targeted by a competitor and analyse the ranking (e.g. SEMrush). You can then assess if there are any other words missing which you are interested in.

As part of this process you need to be mindful of what your competitors do in relation to change. If they have changed something and you notice it, think about why they have done this and how well you believe it is (or isn't) going to work, then monitor it! Although you won't have access to data, you will be able to monitor trends in the marketplace. There are a number of tools that you can use to help with this including Google Trends, Twitter Trending Topics etc.

Finally, look at the topics a competitor discusses on their website and who shared them on social media. You will then gain an insight into validating what might – and might not – work for you.

Chapter summary

This chapter has looked at practical ways you can develop a move to trade internationally. This is best achieved by taking time to prepare the elements you will need to support your goals. It includes researching your target market and being flexible in your approach in order to compete with multinational companies. It involves thinking about the best ways to communicate to your new target audience and the language and cultural differences that exist.

You need to develop an international marketing strategy that is incorporated into your domestic one. It should include factors which are unique to an international market so that you can adapt these and work out how to deal with them.

Finally, look at ways in which you can monitor your progress and the marketing data analytics you need to measure outcomes. This applies to both search engines and social media networks. Also, keep up to date with what your competitors are doing so that you are in a better position to respond to changes they might make.

Key points

✓ Set out a strategy to compete internationally and research your target markets

✓ Focus on what differentiates you and what value you offer

✓ Think carefully about how to develop an international marketing strategy

✓ Put a measurement process in place and monitor your progress

✓ Think about how to monitor competitor activity

NINE

THE FUTURE OF DIGITAL MARKETING

CHAPTER TOPICS

- The power of data

- Machine learning and artificial intelligence

- Augmented reality and future trends

Introduction

Future innovations will continue to shape the digital marketing landscape. Developments in technology will continue to give people the ability to view information online more quickly and offer more choice.

This chapter will look at the power of data and how it will continue to underpin important elements of digital marketing. This includes marketers needing to think about how to adapt in order to get the best out of future campaigns. It will focus on the increase of machine learning and artificial intelligence (AI) as ways to communicate with potential customers. The growth in augmented reality (AR) and mobile video will highlight the need to learn from new technology.

Companies will need to scale up their current strategies based on what technology their target audience is using. If this is done in the right way, it will make it easier to capture customer details, deliver creative campaigns and boost an online presence.

Being in a digital era, the choice is to adapt or face more threats from competitors who take the time to understand and invest in future technology. This includes areas like augmented reality (AR) and virtual reality (VR). It also involves keeping up with trends in the digital marketing arena. Companies who plan and execute improved digital marketing strategies and campaigns are more likely to see a much higher return on their investment (ROI).

The power of data

Although the future of digital marketing will incorporate many changes, one area which is likely to remain constant is the need for collecting and analysing data. This involves an understanding of buyer behaviour and, from this, tailoring the right messages in marketing campaigns to attract interest which can turn into positive buying decisions. Data analytics can increase marketers' focus on the more quantitative element of the interpretation of data (covered in more detail in *Chapter 6, Getting the best out of data analytics*).

It is the combination of this with Qualitative Data Analysis (QDA), however, which is most likely to be a winning formula for interpreting the success of future post-marketing campaigns. With the development of the Web, many of the limitations seen in traditional forms of marketing have disappeared. The question is how far can the Web take us in terms of data analytics?

With the increased speed of transferring data, it is now much easier to upload and transfer documents. This improves the user experience in terms of viewing website pages and makes data collection quicker and easier for marketers. Data storage is another area which, in the future, could become almost unlimited and this is likely to come with lower costs. Real-time mobile apps are likely to be used more as potential customers expect information to be accessed more quickly and 'on the go'.

Technology is one of the key differentiators in terms of how digital marketing can develop and change. People should see data as a new currency, i.e. without it you can't target the right audience and prepare for revenue generation from it in the future. The more relevant data you can gather as to digital activity, including online and mobile, the more you will be able to channel people towards your brand(s).

For companies targeting the B2B market, it makes it easier to understand the business profile of future customers. In a B2C market, it makes it easier to look at social profiles by learning about family purchasing choices and consumer tastes. Knowing this can help you prepare online activity in order to present attractive products to tie in with customers potential needs. As technology evolves, companies will start to build AI into this.

As digital marketers are becoming better able to personalise someone's potential purchasing needs, this makes the actual buying experience more individual and relevant. This is likely to continue making companies become more partner-focused. Better sophistication in data capture and presentation will help to transform the potential business relationships between buyer and seller regardless of whether this is in a B2B or B2C market.

Companies will start to think more in multi-segmented ways to capture different messages that potential buyers want to hear. This data will help to personalise the user experience even more and make it easier to sell to a target audience.

Predictive analytics

Predictive analytics is where statistics are used, often in relation to machine learning. This can be applied to digital marketing in terms of customer preferences. Knowing what future trends interest potential customers is of great interest to marketers. Predictive analytics is not new, but the way future digital marketing will apply it is likely to become more sophisticated. This means gaining a more complete insight into a potential buyer's needs and the rationale for making a particular buying decision.

To support this, companies will need to collect and make sense of the data they have in both B2B and B2C markets. This can be achieved by better data integration in order to get a single view of how particular customers like to be sold to and what type of products and services they need. This also helps to better define the types of customers you don't want! You can create personas to look at this in order to make this differentiation.

The improvement in machine learning, AI and data collection will improve the ability of companies to use analytics with more precision. This should help enormously in relation to predictions about budget spend and conversion rates.

Data analytics has progressed significantly since its inception. Marketing departments have gone from trying to understand the outcomes of a traditional marketing campaign to being able to use statistics and data to make more accurate predictions. This in turn helps to determine both the budget needed to fund a digital marketing campaign and the likely ROI from it.

The following illustration shows the development of marketing data analytics and how it has become more sophisticated. It gives examples of how the development of marketing reporting has progressed in the last four decades. This is particularly significant since the development of the Web.

DEVELOPMENT OF PREDICTIVE ANALYTICS

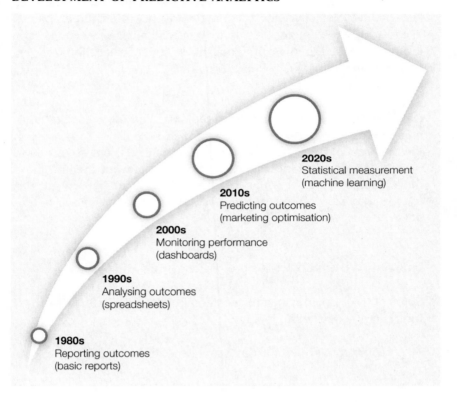

2020s
Statistical measurement
(machine learning)

2010s
Predicting outcomes
(marketing optimisation)

2000s
Monitoring performance
(dashboards)

1990s
Analysing outcomes
(spreadsheets)

1980s
Reporting outcomes
(basic reports)

Other potential trends in the future could include learning more about patterns and preferences in B2B and B2C markets in order to develop better strategies to sell in them; for example:

- A 'data as a service' model

- Ever faster data services

- An increase in the volume of data

- Improved business analytics software

- Better tools for analysis

This will all help to improve the way in which digital marketing uses knowledge. Predictive analytics is already being used: companies like Netflix, for example, use it to help predict alternative choices for customers based on their previous 'likes' of particular films/movies. It also helps studio decisions about the types of films that future customers would like to watch.

Data can be collected and interpreted and used for areas like optimising bids for advertisers. This can then be analysed to establish the best cost options. It can also be used in advertisement targeting on a user search engine which can help to work out the likelihood that a user will click on a particular advert. This enables companies to work out what type of product mix to use when targeting potential customers.

Proving yourself as a real value provider

Some of the ways in which the customer experience is likely to affect future digital marketing include:

- Differentiation of products and services

- A strong focus on maintaining customers

- Developing strong business relationships

- Personalisation of products and service

- Looking at ways to expand mobile services and communication

- Artificial intelligence

Marketers will need to appreciate that as their ability to become more sophisticated in the area of data capture grows, so do a customer's choices and awareness! Getting this right and providing quicker and better communication will help you to keep customers loyal.

An increase in social media usage will improve a user's ability to read and share information and communicate in real time. This, combined with the growth of mobile technology, will present new challenges to marketers, including thinking more carefully about any pre-sales engagement and how to retain customers after they have made a purchase. In a B2B market, this is already covered to some extent by good account management but, in a B2C market, a post-sales relationship can be much more challenging to develop.

This might be more obvious to a multinational company with the resources to deal with post-sales analysis and good account management practices, but many SMEs might not have the financial resources or be prepared for the amount of time needed to keep customers happy and engaged.

However, by using their own CRM and data processing systems well, companies should be in a position to collect and manage both quantitative and qualitative data from customers. Marketers will need to produce imaginative and relevant digital marketing campaigns, with great products and services which meet a customer's needs, in order to offer real value and differentiation.

Creating a marketing ecosystem

By collecting the right data and using it well, the relationship with customers can become more of a two-way engagement. Better market intelligence will mean that a supplier knows more about a potential buyer's needs before that company (in a B2B market) or individual (in a B2C market) thinks about a potential purchase. This level of sophistication is now possible and companies often list people's preferences and act upon them.

The ability of marketers to focus more strongly on someone's needs will change the traditional type of relationship that has existed between buyer and seller. It will make it easier for marketers to know how and when to target their potential audience. It creates a more consultative type of business relationship and discourages one which might, in the past, have been more commodity-based, i.e. one-off purchases.

Social media platforms can play a part as companies look to drive a single corporate message for brand consistency. This is possible with the advance of data and technology and is something which is already being promoted with the use of machine learning and AI.

Machine learning and artificial intelligence

Machine learning is where technology platforms learn to do something themselves rather than being instructed. It can be used for applications like data-mining, that is, examining large amounts of data to try and find previously undiscovered relationships within it. It can also be used for the recognition of images, language processing and advanced systems. Gaming is also a popular application of machine learning.

AI, however, is the ability of computers and machines to learn tasks normally associated with humans. This includes language, problem-solving, perception and, most importantly, decision-making. True AI resembles human behaviour in the sense that it reacts to what it learns. It then makes connections based on that new knowledge. The more it learns, the more intelligent it gets. Let us look at the type of structure used to underpin an AI model. This can be illustrated in the following way:

ARTIFICIAL INTELLIGENCE

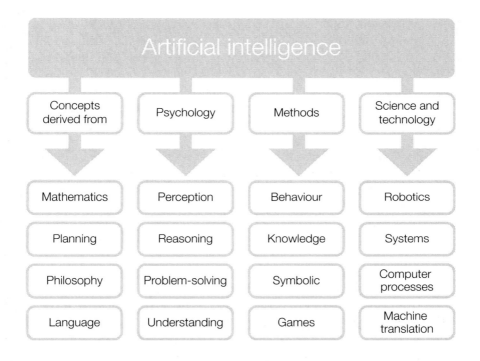

The combination of subjects such as mathematics, science, psychology, language and technology can help to provide outcomes which not only make sense of complex information but also save valuable time. In reality, achieving true AI is still many years away whereas machine learning is already established and is the closest thing we already have.

AI and social media

AI will help companies better interact and respond to their target audience whether B2B or B2C. This will save time in not having to think about and test different scenarios of potential marketing outcomes.

Deep-structured learning is similar to machine learning based on algorithms which look at replicating high level representations of data. This type of social semantics is likely to be used more in the future on social media networks by companies in order to study social behaviour to look for trends. This in turn can then be fed back for marketing purposes to identify products and services which might be attractive to particular groups of people.

Microsoft tried this with its computer-programmed AI 'chatbot', Tay, which tried to simulate intelligent and learned conversation. The company opened a Twitter account to test the interaction on social media but, within hours of it being launched, Tay began to communicate abusive and controversial messages. This was instigated through 'trolls' (people looking for shock and conflict in web conversations) and had to be taken offline (*The Guardian*, 30 March 2016).

Although Tay was clearly not advanced enough yet to interact at this level, it does show that this type of AI is closer to becoming a reality on a large scale in the future. It also demonstrates the risk involved in delegating this type of activity to a computer programme.

AI will help companies to understand and disseminate the marketing message across their audience segments, personas and demographics. It will decide the best way and time to reach someone on social media and will also be aware of where someone is in a particular area of a country or region. Eric Schmidt, the Executive Chairman of Alphabet, parent company of Google, said: 'Our tools will get better and better at getting the right ad in the right place ... in these new architectures.' (I/O conference, 2016).

Social television viewing and second screening (where younger viewers are now more likely to be using a tablet at the same time as watching television) will change the way marketers target them. The combination of AI and social media will help marketers progress communication to users about their brands to encourage continued recognition and adoption.

SEO and PPC in relation to AI

Search Engine Optimisation (SEO) is another area which is changing and being influenced by AI. In the past, companies would often build a website and get some backlinks (when one company links their website to another) to create authority. That would improve the chances of getting a higher ranking in a Google search. As these methods started to be manipulated by SEO specialists, search engines like Google kept updating their algorithms. This made them more contextually aware, which helped to better understand the content.

Google has brought out RankBrain, a machine-learning AI system which tries to understand the content and context of a website. This is likely to change the future of SEO as it is designed to try and remove keyword density (the amount of times a keyword appears on a website page). This helps a user to establish how relevant a particular website might be.

RankBrain helps with areas like content marketing, which are potentially more useful to a marketer than a blog. With content marketing, you should look at categorisation and keep related content easily accessible. This will make it easier in a Google search for your website pages to be more relevant to potential users.

As part of this type of change, marketers should do some competitive analysis to see how other companies gain authority, i.e. in relation to how many times search results appear. You should also brand your content on sites like YouTube, LinkedIn and SlideShare so that people look on these social media networks and find your company's website more easily.

One of the ways to build traffic initially is to pay for certain keywords in a search engine, which can be done by using Pay Per Click (PPC) to make them more specific. With AI in the future, you will be able to add more keywords and phrases in order to optimise any search. This might lead to more bidding for keywords with intent, i.e. a longer, more detailed number of words being used. This could include questions like 'what is the cost of x?'

This will help companies optimise their investment in PPC with the use of a search engine. From a different perspective, AI will help advertisers better relate their messages to the keywords searched by a potential customer/consumer.

AI and customer service

Another area where AI is developing is pro-active customer service. The topic of customer service in relation to marketing is covered in *Chapter 3, Changes that impact on the customer experience*. Saffron, a division of Intel, is developing technology for US finance company USAA which will look to predict when a customer might want to get in touch with a supplier and the reason for this (*MIT Technology Review*, 28 March 2016).

It could be used to help plan the types of resources needed to supply a high level of customer service and to predict when customers might want to make a purchase. This technology can be applied to different markets and is something which is likely to grow in terms of demand and efficiency. The concept of machine learning and AI helping to make the future of digital marketing easier can also be seen with the potential of web design.

Automated web design

In the future, websites are more likely to be created automatically. You are starting to see the integration of AI with website design. For example, The Grid (an automated AI website builder) uses a number of features which make it better able to be intuitive to potential users (thegrid.io). These include:

- Face detection in photos

- Optical character recognition (OCR)

- Formal and informal use of fonts

- Drag and drop layout

- Colour matching

This type of design allows a website to be designed without human intervention in a very short period of time. As the dynamics of a build can be easily changed, i.e. font colour and size, this type of technology has the ability to make future web design quick and intuitive.

In digital marketing terms, AI offers fully automated software which will enhance areas like:

- Websites

- Video

- Email marketing

- E-commerce

- Social media

- Search engines

This can be illustrated in the following way:

ARTIFICIAL INTELLIGENCE USE FOR TRACKING DIGITAL MARKETING

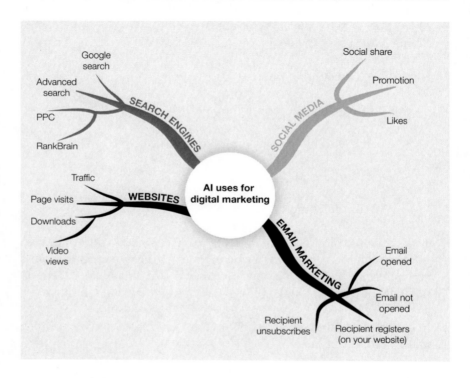

AI can also help with areas like e-commerce where it can 'learn' a company's purchasing process and a consumer's tastes from website views and purchasing history. This can then be used to remember consumer preferences in order to create a unique set of needs for each shopper.

AI's advanced functionality will be able to make elements of digital marketing more intuitive. Speech and language recognition are already being used as part of machine learning and, in the future, there are likely to be greater advances in understanding more complex levels of interpretation. This type of progress will help marketers to make better use of unstructured information in order to improve brand targeting.

Augmented reality and future trends

Augmented reality (AR) is a real-time view of computer-generated sensory information in order to create a real-world environment. To achieve this, it overlays text, audio, video and graphics on physical objects to provide information and images in real time. AR enables a user to gain the combination of a digital and physical experience. Virtual reality (VR) is not the same; it involves simulation of a real, three-dimensional (3D) environment, creating an artificial experience using a computer monitor or headset.

AR is not a new type of technology; apps use it, but it is progressing in terms of digital marketing purposes. It enables customers to share the experience of a purchase with a supplier in a more personal way. Marketers are already using AR to gain potential customers by asking them to register the application of the enhancement they view. This enables them to track its use to get an understanding of the length and number of interactions. AR has several advantages for digital marketing because:

- It can be relatively inexpensive

- It is interactive

- It has the potential to offer a different dimension for digital marketing campaigns

- It has trackable results

- It can offer repeatable engagement with its target audience

AR can also help to increase brand awareness, partly because its use is still relatively new. By using it in marketing campaigns, companies will be able to give users more information and an alternative way to interact with their brands. It also helps to promote the blend of the digital marketing and real-life experience. This is something which should increase a user's awareness and attraction to a particular brand.

The forecast of sales in relation to AR was predicted to exceed $150 billion by 2020, although this was later revised down to $120 billion (Digi-Capital, AR/VR forecast, January 2016). Companies like Google and Facebook are investing in this technology, for example:

- **Google Glass** – an optical head-mounted display designed in the shape of eye glasses but hands-free

- **Magic Leap** – a head-mounted virtual retinal display, mixing virtual objects with real-world images

- **Oculus** – offers a VR head-mounted display designed for video gaming, purchased by Facebook in 2014

- **HoloLens** – a head-mounted display from Microsoft which runs AR applications

Social media could be a good match with AR through shared content and brand connections, increasing the chances of sales. Other likely ways in which AR will continue to be developed in the future include:

- Its use in shops

- 'On the go' apps

- High street marketing

- Advertising for gaming

- Commerce and many consumer products

- Education, military and industrial applications

To support this, AR can help potential buyers take virtual tours of buildings and holiday destinations to promote a potential experience. Another huge market for AR is the mobile user. Mobile devices are set to grow from 7.3 billion users to about 9 billion by 2021 and subscriptions are set to double in size to over 6 billion from 2015 to 2020. From this type of prediction, you can see the huge potential for AR and mobile (Ericsson Mobility Report, Ericsson, June 2015).

Although still in its infancy, AR offers a completely new way of advertising. It isn't an exact science when predicting the future of AR and VR; however, Goldman Sachs estimates that by 2025 the AR market will reach £80 billion worldwide, approximately the same size as the current PC market (Goldman Sachs Global Investment Research).

However, some analysts think the market could be at least twice as big as this. Even if the lower predictions here are accurate, it gives an indication of its potential and why marketers should look at ways of including it in their digital marketing strategies.

The growth of mobile video and other future trends

Another predicted area of future growth is that of mobile video (much of which can be used in conjunction with AR and VR). Many large companies are already in a good position to take advantage of the growth in mobile users due to their size and resources, but SMEs might not be.

If a company doesn't have a dedicated marketing team, it can take more time and cost to adapt to changing trends. This is why taking the time to think about how your digital marketing strategy can adapt to changes in mobile and technology will enable you to better prepare for the future.

Mobile video marketing is likely to be one trend which marketers will be able to target. People using mobile phones are more likely to watch video advertisements if they are interactive, interesting, relevant or amusing. Many potential consumers use mobile devices to help them make purchasing decisions. The convenience of using a mobile phone or tablet is much higher than someone using a desktop device or watching television. That is why the potential of mobile video is worth investing in.

Marketers should look at developing some type of mobile video marketing as part of their overall digital marketing strategy. A video on a mobile device can increase the social experience someone has, especially as many viewings will be outside a user's working hours. The type of areas to focus on in relation to mobile video, that you should consider, include:

- Which demographic groups are potential targets

- The types of mobile devices that users are likely to have

- How you can you connect with your target audience

- What video platforms you should use

- What type of content you should consider

- How to measure these types of campaigns

With mobile video, if you can communicate a relevant and engaging short film, you increase the chances of connecting with your target audience. Also, think about how much content can be shared on social media networks to assess its potential.

Other areas which are likely to grow in the future include:

- A stronger focus on content marketing

- Marketing automation

- Digital personalisation

- Separation between local and global marketing trends

- More apps which support different markets

- E-commerce

Consider what you need to do to ensure that your brand(s) stand out in order to create interest and value. Also, think about how you can adapt your digital marketing campaigns in the future to reflect trends and changes to digital technology. By doing so, you are more likely to be at the 'cutting edge' of developments which can give you a USP and help to achieve the ROI you are looking for.

KEY QUESTIONS

- What AI, AR and VR do you think could help you in the future?

- How much do you know about mobile video and its potential?

Chapter summary

The future of digital marketing innovations like AI has been high-lighted in this chapter. Most of them are already in existence in some way. However, it is how companies adapt to the changes involved in their use that will help determine their success in dealing with the future elements of technology within digital marketing.

As technology improves, the ability to collect, interpret and store data also improves. This will mean a change in the way companies gain an understanding of future customer needs and choices. Marketers will be better able to use information that comes from areas like predictive analytics to fine-tune their research and campaigns. This will make targeted marketing easier to deliver and help brands to be seen as more innovative.

The increase in areas like AI and AR change the landscape in marketing terms and the balance between traditional and digital marketing. Areas like mobile video will add to a potential customer's ability to access brands in an interactive way. The future of digital marketing is about how to improve techniques in order to deliver exciting and relevant products and services.

Knowing which types of technology to invest in and how to get the best out of them is a challenge that companies face in order to achieve their growth potential. Getting this right will help to increase brand awareness, sales performance and customer retention.

Key points

✓ Think about how you can manage the data you collect for marketing purposes

✓ Look at how technology can be used to improve your digital marketing

✓ Take the time to think about how machine learning, AI and AR can help you

✓ Do research on how digital marketing is changing so that you keep up with it

✓ Think about how you can take advantage of the growth in mobile
   video technology

TEN
BIBLIOGRAPHY

ONE A brief history of digital marketing

* Number of Internet users worldwide, 2016 – statistica.com

* Globalisation of products and their higher level of homogenisation – The Globalization of Markets, T Levitt, *Harvard Business Review*, 1983

THREE Changes that impact on the customer experience

* Digitizing customer care – McKinsey, eCare customer survey 2012

* Net Promoter Score® NPS – registered trademark of Fred Reichheld, Bain & Company and Satmetrix

* Internetretailing.net – Forrester data report: Online retail forecast, 2016 – 2021 (Western Europe)

FOUR Getting your website to add value

* UK small companies with five employees or fewer don't have a website – Redshift Research, 2015

* Survey of how many small businesses would recommend having a website – Verisign, 2015

- Search engines – Google, Bing, Yahoo, Ask AOL – Alexa Global Traffic Rank and US Traffic Rank – Compete and Quantcast, February, 2016

FIVE Platforms for digital marketing communication

- Growth in social media sites – information from a combination of public-domain related websites including pewinternet.org, smartinsights.com, emarketer.com

- Revenue from the top social media sites – emarketer.com

- Social media users, 2016 – a combination of nuancedmedia.com, smartinsights.com, brandwatch.com, linkedin.com, twitter.com, facebook.com, youtube.com, forbes.com, nielsen.com (2014), instagram.com, pinterest.com

- Number of LinkedIn users, 2016 – statista.com

- Other sources include webtrends.about.com, smallbiztrends.com, ebizmba.com, facebook.com, twitter.com, youtube.com, instagram.com, pinterest.com

- Social media networks global advertising revenue, 2016 – statista.com

- For other social networks mentioned, websites can be found by adding .com as a suffix with the exception of plusgoogle.com

SIX Getting the best out of data analytics

- Various sources used for Google Analytics dashboard including thenextweb.com, econsultancy.com, wurlwind.co.uk

- For other data analytics software mentioned, websites can be found by adding .com as a suffix with the exception of commun.it, hootsuite.com, pro.iconosquare.com, moz.com, getpocket.com and marinsoftware.co.uk

- Responsive web design – google.com

- Measuring the level of social influence – klout.com

- Who do we trust? – Global Trust in Advertising survey 2015, Nielsen, neilsen.com

SEVEN Integrating with traditional forms of marketing

- The Marketing Mix – Neil H Borden, 1953

- US total media ad spending share by media, 2016 – emarketer.com

- Television advertising global revenue prediction – statista.com

NINE The future of digital marketing

- Microsoft Tay computer programme – *The Guardian*, 30 March 2016

- Machine learning and AI – Eric Schmidt, Executive Chairman of Alphabet (parent company of Google), I/O conference, 2016

- Predictive websites – The Grid, thegrid.io

- Use of AI in predicting future customer proactivity – *MIT Technology Review*, 28 March 2016, technologyreview.com

- AR future predicted sales – Digi-Capital, AR/VR forecast, January 2016

- AR future predicted mobile users and subscriptions – Ericsson Mobility Report, Ericsson, June 2015

- Future market of AR and VR – Goldman Sachs Global Investment Research, January 2016

NOTES

23/1/18